Horses' Teeth

Horses' Teeth

Prevention – Recognition – Treatment

Dr. Kai Kreling

THE LYONS PRESS

Guilford, Connecticut
An imprint of the Globe Pequot Press

Copyright © 2004 by The Lyons Press

First published as *Zahnprobleme bei Pferden* by Cadmos Verlag in 1998.

The Lyons Press is an imprint of The Globe Pequot Press.

10 9 8 7 6 5 4 3 2 1

Printed in Germany.

Translated by Desiree Gerber
Designed by Ravenstein Brain Pool, Berlin
Photographs by Dr. Kai Kreling
Drawings by Michaela Heitmann
Cartoons by Gerrit Kreling

ISBN 1-59228-696-8

Library of Congress Cataloging-in-Publication data is available on file.

Contents

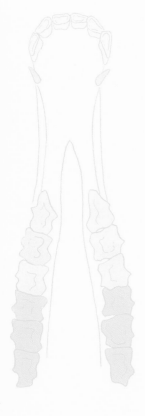

5 Examination of the Teeth and Mouth – When, How and Why? 82

Dentistry for Horses

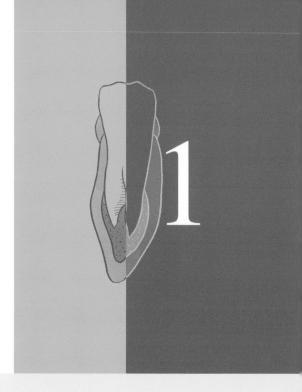

1

Writing a book about horses' teeth may sound slightly unusual at first. It is only when you get more closely involved that the realization strikes that too little consideration is given to the teeth of horses. The horse's teeth are life-preserving tools. The chewing surfaces of the molars grind big food particles into digestible sizes. If this system ceases to function, it can promptly lead to starvation, decreased performance and dramatic illnesses.

In view of their vital importance, it is only correct to say that horses' teeth should be given more consideration. This does not mean brushing on a daily basis, but regular inspection of the teeth and mouth. As humans, we normally have our teeth examined once or twice a year, even though the life-preserving significance is largely absent in our case. After all, we can happily eat with dentures if we lose all our teeth.

The tooth of the horse is constructed in such a way that the visible crown of the tooth above the gum is but a small part of the whole tooth, most of which is embedded in

Tooth care for horses?

the jawbone. The tooth is ground down and shortened with time, and the reserve of the tooth erupts accordingly.

It is not only bad feed and obvious pain that cause problems in the mouth: many other illnesses that are at first not classified as teeth problems can also have an influence on the health of the horse's mouth. There are hundreds of frustrated riders who have horses that are unhappy in their work due to problems with their teeth. This can result in the riders making unreasonable demands on the horses and expecting them to do things that are impossible mainly as a result of the pain they experience. In this situation, achieving a harmonious mode of riding will be out of the question.

There are many direct health complications as a result of teeth problems: weight loss, poor appetite, drop in performance, blockage of the pharynx and recurring colics are the most frequent symptoms. These complications can often be resolved relatively easily and will quickly improve the horse's quality of life, not to mention relieving the owner!

Localizing a problem of the mouth can be difficult at the best of times, however. Connecting it with riding problems, recurring colics, blockage of the pharynx, poor feeding and inferior performance is often even more difficult. The aim of this book is to inform the rider and horse owner about the health of the horse's mouth and how to detect possible problems of the mouth and teeth at an early stage. The first course of action is described. For further treatment the help of your veterinarian should be enlisted. The fundamental anatomical and physiological principles will be discussed in the following chapters.

The Horse's Teeth

What teeth do horses have?

Horses have four groups of teeth:

  1: Incisors

  2: Canines

  3: Premolars

  4: Molars

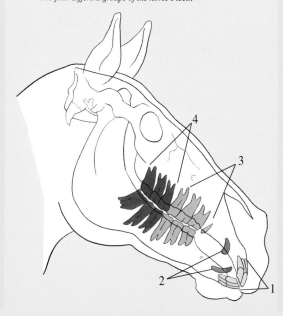

The four different groups of the horse's teeth

The teeth are classified according to function and form. The incisors are at the front of the mouth where it opens. There are six incisors in the upper and six in the lower jaw of every adult horse. Their function is the prehension and cutting of food.

The canines are found within one or two centimeters of the incisors, further towards the back of the mouth. These teeth are also called stallion or gelding teeth. Naming them like this is slightly misleading, for they are not exclusively found in stallions or geldings. They are, however, often found in the male animal and seldom in the female. Canines are regressed defense teeth, originally used for fighting and still very apparent in dogs and cats. The canines have no real purpose anymore in the domesticated horse.

The most important teeth are the molars. The first molar is approximately 5-6 cm behind the canines.

The bit lies in the toothless space between the canines and the molars. This space is called the diastema. The word is from the Greek for "space between," meaning interdental space. In the narrow sense of the word, every space between teeth is called an interdental space.

In the horse's mouth the molars are so close together that the concept of interdental space between them is limited. The molars can be divided into the first three, called premolars or front cheek teeth, and the three directly following, called the molars or cheek teeth. In the upper jaw, sometimes also in the lower jaw, one will frequently find a small tooth directly in front of the first premolar. This tooth is called the "wolf tooth" and is the subsidiary remnant of a tooth. In the ancestors of our horses, these teeth were functional, but with evolution they have become superfluous.

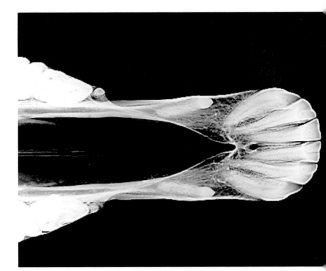

X-ray of a top jaw from above and the side. The canines and the wolf teeth are clearly visible.

What is particular to horses' teeth?

Teeth, especially the molars, are functional chewing surfaces. The movement of a horse's jaws grinds food into small pieces. This grinding action also causes the teeth to become worn. Continual eruption of a horse's teeth results in the surfaces always being replaced. The visible tooth that protrudes from the gum is in fact only 10-15 percent of the actual tooth in a young horse. This part of the tooth is called the visible crown. In humans the teeth that are visible are also called the crowns. The human tooth is brachydont (tooth with a short crown) while the horse's tooth is hypsodont (tooth with a long crown).

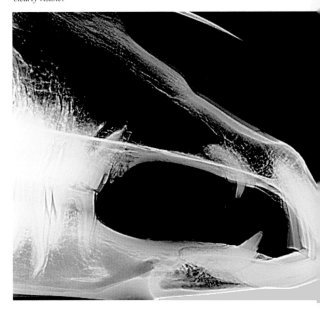

The human tooth is strong enough, in the circumstances of normal human nutrition, to last a lifetime, or at least a substantial part of the human life, in order to grind the food into smaller particles.

The chewing surfaces of horses' teeth are under great pressure due to the normal diet of tough food,

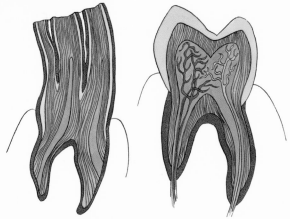

The human tooth, right, is described as brachydont, as it only has a short crown. The horse's tooth (left) is hypsodont. The long crown of the young horse lies mainly in the jawbone and is ground off throughout life. It erupts continuously.

fed in big portions. This grinds down the tooth substance, and the rest of the crown erupts continuously. If the crown does not erupt, the tooth will be ground down completely, and the horse will starve

to death without teeth. This mechanism of continual eruption is a peculiarity of horses' teeth, to keep the horse well nourished throughout life. The nutrition of the modern horse, however, means that this occurrence can cause several problems. These will be discussed in the chapters on diseases of the teeth and mouth.

How did the modern horse's teeth develop?

The Latin term for the modern horse as we know it is *Equus caballus*. The ancestors of the horse developed from the Eohippus, which lived in South America 50 to 70 million years ago. The Eohippus lived on easily digested, protein-rich plants, mainly a diet of leaves. The teeth of the Eohippus were mainly brachydont (short crowns).

Evolution of modern horses from the Eohippus, the primitive horse with three toes.

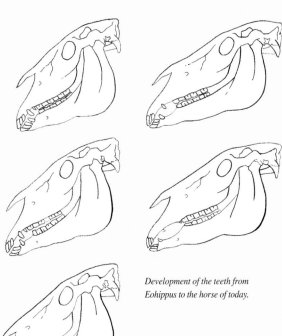

Development of the teeth from Eohippus to the horse of today.

As a rule of thumb, one can assume that doubling the body weight will increase the energy requirements at least eight times. This means the energy requirements of the evolving horse increased many times over. Apart from the changes in the physical size of the body and the digestive system, the technique of ingestion had to change. Nutrition was not taken from a tree at eye level anymore. Prairie grass was now the new feed. The neck developed to a greater length in order for the horse to reach the grass, which was not as nutritious as the leaves. The result was that more time was needed to ingest grass to equal the requirement of energy. The assumption is made that the Eohippus spent 3-4 hours a day feeding. The inhabitant of the prairie increased this to an average of 16 hours a day. To top it all, the grass had a much tougher structure than the soft leaves of the trees, and the low energy content of the grass necessitated an obvious enlargement of the chewing surfaces to ensure optimum preparation for the process of digestion. At the same time the head of the horse developed into a longer form to accommodate the bigger teeth in the mouth. A tough challenge was made on the teeth with the long hours of grinding. To compensate for this, the brachydont teeth developed into hypsodont teeth with long crowns. This meant that the teeth could accommodate the wear, and the result of this was a much longer lifetime. The incisors also turned into long hypsodont teeth, making it easier to cut short grass and even the roots of grasses without the early loss of the teeth.

These teeth are comparable to those of the cat, dog or human. It was not necessary for the teeth substance to keep on erupting, for their food sources were not tough but easily ground. This meant that the chewing surfaces were not heavily used. In the course of time, the climate and the vegetation changed. Jungle and forest landscapes became prairie. The Eohippus developed and changed with the land- scape. The dog-sized, three-toed primitive horse turned into the bigger, one-toed horse, as we know it today. The body weight of the modern horse is two to three times that of the primitive horse.

The rough chewing surface of the cheek teeth is plain to see.

The chewing surface developed a rough, terraced profile, and this helped in the grinding of food. The terraces and roughness of the chewing surfaces are the result of three substances with different degrees of hardiness. The softer material is ground away

The sideways movement of the lower jaw against the upper jaw in this photo is the equivalent of the breadth of one incisor.

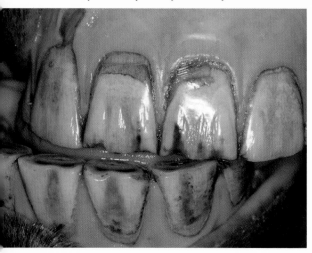

more rapidly than the tough matter, and thus the chewing surface develops cutting differences between the substances. The resilient and irregular surfaces working together with the strong muscles of mastication are extremely efficient in breaking up food particles. This means one has to be very careful when examining a horse's mouth. The mechanics of the horse's mouth have the potential to cause serious injury to fingers.

Biting on food only accounts for partial breaking up of the food particles. The joint of the jaw has adapted to the change of nourishment as well. This joint not only opens up and down like a hinge, but also allows for a particularly effective sideways movement of the lower jaw against the upper jaw. This enables a circular movement of the lower jaw that functions as a rasp, grating and grinding food into small particles.

Construction and Function of the Teeth and Their Surroundings

What does a horse's tooth consist of?

Enamel

Enamel is the hardest substance in the body. It is 95-98 percent inorganic material. This means that there are no cells found in this substance, but a high proportion of minerals. Enamel is colorless and only looks white because of the white dentine beneath it. There is only 4 percent water in enamel, which makes it extremely brittle. Due to this small percentage of water and the high percentage of minerals, it is also called "dead substance." The body cannot repair enamel that has been destroyed. The microstructure of enamel has big crystals, bigger than those of dentine, cement and even bone. There is a dense filling material between the crystals, and the combination of these two substances produces the hardness and brittleness of the tooth.

Dentine

The biggest part of the tooth is made up of dentine. This consists of 70 percent inorganic material, 20 percent organic matter and 5 percent water. Dentine is "alive" and sensitive to a degree. Humans can distinguish between warm and cold sensations through the nerves that supply the dentine. Experience has shown that these sensations are all but absent in the horse. When a horse's teeth are floated, extreme heat can be generated if insufficient water is used to rinse, but fortunately most horses seem to tolerate this. This means that the sensitivity of the enamel is exceedingly poor. The dentine has the capacity to repair certain defects and has the advantage that it is not as brittle as enamel, which means the danger of injury and damage is reduced.

Dentine is made up of little tubes, filled with secondary dentine towards the chewing surface. Secondary dentine is a material that repairs the tooth

Dentine is made up of little tubes, which become filled with secondary dentine towards the chewing surface.

where it has been ground or broken off. This mechanism protects the body from bacterial infection via the tooth. Dentine is a pale-yellow to creamy color.

Cement

Cement is the softest material of the tooth. It is made of 45-50 percent inorganic material, 45-50 percent organic material and up to 10 percent water. Cement has a yellow color. The structure of cement is very similar to that of bone, and it is relatively flexible due to the high percentage of organic material. Cement produces the so-called fibers of Sharpey, which hold the teeth in position in the socket, acting like anchors.

The socket has structures that nurture the tooth. The cement makes its surface available for this purpose. This connection is flexible, to accommodate the continuous eruption of the tooth. The way this works is that there is an ongoing buildup and break down of cement through the horse's life, ensuring that there is always a stable connection between tooth and socket.

The less mineralized cement on the outside of the tooth absorbs pigments from food, thus staining the tooth brown. This discoloration has no bearing on the health of the tooth.

The cement gives extra protection to the dentine in the area of the root. In very old horses, where the teeth have become extremely shortened, only dentine and cement remain as a chewing surface. Old horses will rapidly grind down their teeth, and this is why their teeth are often called "soft" or "rubber" denticles.

The building blocks of a horse's tooth

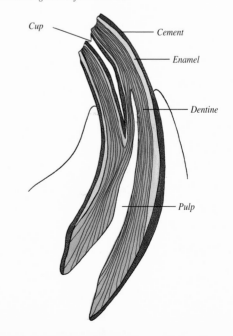

Cup

Cement

Enamel

Dentine

Pulp

Construction of the tooth and the anatomical structures

> *Crown*
> *Root*
> *Pulp*
> *Socket*
> *Chewing surface*

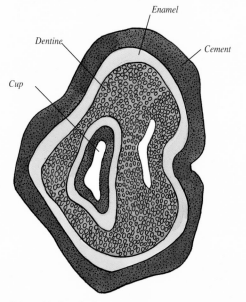

Cross section through a horse's tooth

Dentine

Enamel

Cement

Cup

The crown

The crown is the part of the tooth that lies above the root. The part of the tooth that is visible in the mouth above the level of the gum is known as the visible crown. The part of the tooth beneath the level of the gum up to the root of the tooth is the reserve crown. The transition between the visible and reserve crown is flush. In humans the part of the tooth embraced by the gum is called the neck of the tooth. Due to the continuous eruption of the tooth in horses, there is no real neck of the tooth. Deciduous teeth have a narrowing of the crown around the gum margin. This could be called the neck of the tooth, but the term is not used in practice. The crown is made of three building blocks. Dentine is the main ingredient of the tooth. Enamel, the hardest substance, surrounds the dentine, and a thin layer of cement covers the enamel.

The root

The root is the rest of the tooth that joins onto the crown. The root anchors the tooth in the bottom of the jawbone or rises into the sinuses. The root of the tooth consists of dentine and cement.

Old horses that have used their entire available tooth will wear out the roots. This will be a rapid process because the hard substance, the enamel, is not present in the root.

The pulp

The pulp is the supply network of the tooth. This network reaches the pulp canal through an opening at the tip of the root, and this way supplies the pulp of the tooth with the necessary nutrients. Each tooth has at least one pulp canal; the molars have two to three per tooth, and these can have two to three evaginations in the tooth. The roots of the molars are completed by two years of age. The pulp canal develops until the fifth to sixth year.

The tooth of the horse gets worn out during its life. The pulp canal gets pushed upwards or downwards into the mouth. In order to stop the open canal from becoming a highway for infection, there is a secondary layer of dentine that closes the canal once it opens in the mouth. In the secondary incisors the dental star will be visible, this being the pulp canal filled with secondary dentine. The opening at the tip of the root of the tooth, with the nerves, blood supply and other tissue, stays open until the horse's seventh or eighth year. Up to this point there is a steady production of tooth substance. After eight years the teeth will erupt continuously and be ground down at the chewing surface.

The socket

The socket is the bony formation incorporating the tooth in the jaw of the horse. This socket is lined with a thin membrane that serves both as connection to the tooth and insulation to the mouth. This connection is constantly under construction to keep up with the eruption of the tooth out of the socket.

The chewing surface

The chewing surface of the permanent tooth in the young horse is coated in cement with a thin layer of enamel underneath it. This protective layer gets worn swiftly when the horse chews, exposing the enamel, dentine and cement that lie beneath. The chewing surface wears at a rate of 2-3 mm per year, depending on the diet of the horse. Stabled horses that are fed hay as a base will eat for approximately 13 hours per day. Horses in paddocks where only little and poor grass is available will eat for up to 16 hours per day. The composition of the food will have a big influence on the speed with which the teeth get worn down. Hay or grasses with a high silicate content, solid salts in the stalks or leaves of grasses will all wear the teeth down at a quicker rate than softer food will. The amount of water in the food will also make a difference. Hay is chewed with approximately half the amount of chewing motion needed for fresh grass from the pasture. This will show in the wear of the teeth.

There are other factors that influence the wear of the teeth. The chewing power of the horse, the angle of the surfaces in relation to each other, the shape of the teeth and the mechanics of chewing are all important contributing factors. Toothache and the uneven pattern of wear resulting can change the position of the teeth and lead to unnatural usage.

The surface of the molar is composed of vertical circular folds of enamel and dentine, topped with a layer of cement. The differing degrees of hardness

The top surface of an upper molar. Two segments with their own pits can be seen.

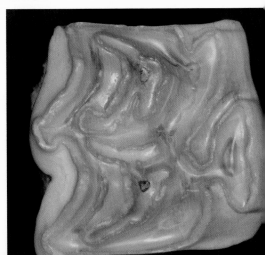

Lower molar   *Upper molar*

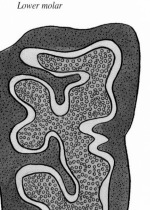
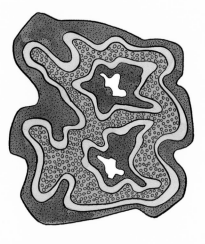

The molar has circular structures composed of enamel and dentine, topped with a layer of cement. The central pits are called infundibulum.

the remains of a canal for the blood vessels while the permanent tooth was still developing. The cup is worn off (by approximately three mm per year) as time goes by. The cup in the lower jaw is around six mm deep, and the cup in the upper jaw is up to twelve mm deep. The cup is gradually worn away to form the mark and this stays visible for a while. The mark is visible in the upper jaw up to the fifteenth year.

of these substances contribute to the uneven wear when chewing. Enamel is extremely hard and does not wear as rapidly as dentine. The layers formed by these differing rates of wear function like rasps. The molars in the upper jaw are almost square and have two segments of enamel and dentine on the chewing surface, each with its own pit. The lower molar teeth are narrower and more rectangular in shape and have only one segment of enamel.

Cup, mark and dental star

In a young and healthy incisor, the cup is an obvious funnel-like depression in the chewing surface. This dimple is

A view of the incisors of the lower jaw. The central incisors (I1) only have the mark visible. The intermediate incisors (I2) show cups of teeth in full contact. The corner incisors (I3) have the distinctive cups of teeth not yet in occlusion.

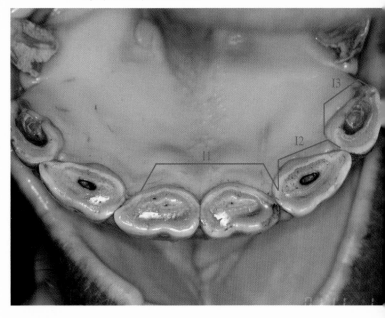

The dental star is a dark or light brown colored spot on the chewing surface more towards the outside of the tooth, that is, the lip side. This is the pulp of the tooth, and unless some provision was made, exposure would be extremely painful; therefore that has been closed up with secondary dentine.

While a hollow of the structures in the tooth forms the cup, the dental star is an elevated cavity filled with secondary dentine. This difference is easy to establish using a fingernail: the enamel of the cup is slightly higher on the niveau of the chewing surface, and a small indent can be felt with the nail. When scratched across the chewing surface of the tooth, the nail gets stuck between the enamel folds. With the dental star, however, the nail does not feel a slight indent, but glides over the top.

Arrangement and development of the teeth in the jaw

The arrangement of teeth per jaw-half	
3 Incisors	in both sides of the upper and lower jaw
1 Canine	(not all horses) in both sides of the upper and lower jaw
1 Wolf tooth	(not all horses) in both sides of the upper jaw, seldom in lower jaw
3 Premolars	in both sides of the upper and lower jaw
3 Molars	in both sides of the upper and lower jaw.

The cup represents the remains of the canal for blood vessels while the tooth was growing. The dental star is the closed pulp canal.

Upper and lower jaws with 6 incisors, 2 canines, (the wolf teeth) and 6 premolars and molars

Development of the tooth with age:

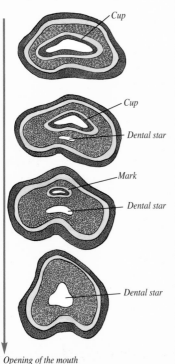

Cup

Cup
Dental star

Mark
Dental star

Dental star

Opening of the mouth

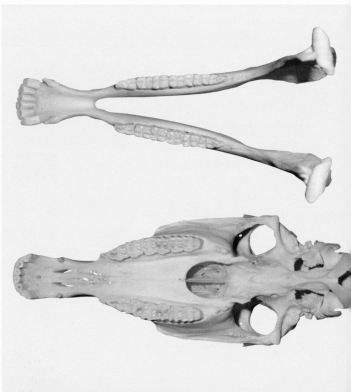

The incisors (front teeth)

The two incisors at the front of the mouth are called central incisors in both the upper and lower jaw. The next is the lateral or intermediate incisor, and the third is called the corner incisor. The first incisors are temporary teeth and are shed to be replaced by permanent incisors. The foal is born with central incisors, or they will erupt within the first days of the foal's life. The laterals develop within four to six weeks after birth, and the corner teeth will appear between six and nine months of age.

> *As a rule of thumb one can say:*
>
> *Eruption of the temporary (deciduous) incisors:*
>
> | | | |
> |---|---|---|
> | *Six days* | = | *centrals break through* |
> | *Six weeks* | = | *laterals break through* |
> | *Six months* | = | *corner teeth break through* |

This can be applied to aid in the aging of foals. The deciduous teeth are smaller and whiter than permanent teeth and are tapered towards the gum. The deciduous teeth have a narrower chewing surface and look like tiny scoops. The permanent teeth erupt on the inside of the deciduous teeth and will push the temporary teeth out. Occasionally the milk teeth do not fall out, and remain stuck next to the permanent teeth. These tooth rests (caps) can easily be removed with tooth forceps, because they have no stabilizing roots and are only held in place by the gum.

The central deciduous incisors will shed at two and a half years, the laterals at three and a half years and the corner teeth at four and a half years. The permanent teeth take roughly six months to emerge in-

to the mouth and to come into wear (level with the adjacent teeth). This means a horse with central incisors out and in wear is three years old. When the intermediates are out and in wear, a horse is four, and once the corner incisors are out and in wear, the horse is five years old. Determining a horse's age between three and five is very easy and extremely reliable.

> *Shedding of incisors*
>
> | | |
> |---|---|
> | *Central* | *out at two and a half and in wear at age three.* |
> | *Intermediate* | *out at three and a half and in wear at age four.* |
> | *Corner* | *out at four and a half and in wear at age five.* |

The incisors of the upper jaw are embedded in the upper jaw, and the incisors of the lower jaw are embedded in the lower jaw. The gum provides additional stability to the teeth. The position of the teeth, when seen in a cross section of the jaw, is semicircular and will change in the life of the horse to an almost straight and horizontal orientation. Seen from the side, the incisors of a young horse are almost perpendicular to each other.

The incisors of the young horse are perpendicular to each other.

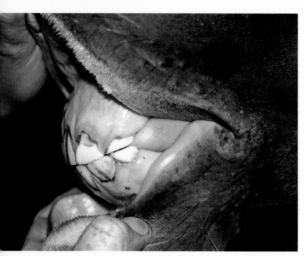

The corner teeth are still milk teeth, centrals and laterals are permanent. A cap (tooth rest) is still visible on the upper lateral. This horse is four years old.

The upper corner tooth is already visible, the smaller white deciduous corner tooth is still detectable in the lower jaw.

Over the course of time the teeth flatten out to slope acutely. The teeth are curved inwards towards the mouth, and the rest of the crown and the roots extend nearly horizontal, relatively far into the bone of the jaw. The chewing surfaces of the incisors in particular are traditionally used to determine age in horses. The shape of the teeth, the position relative to each other, the condition of the chewing surface and the existence of cup and dental star will give an indication of the age of the horse. (See page 31 on aging the horse.)

The canines or tushes

Canines are mainly found in stallions and geldings, but occasionally also in mares. In the lower jaw they are roughly one to two centimeters behind the corner tooth; in the upper jaw they are about two to four centimeters behind the corner tooth. They are formed as deciduous teeth but are too small to break through the gum margin. The permanent teeth appear between the ages of four and six years. They have no chewing surface and are formed in a flattened shape, sometimes tapering to a pointed end. The canine, with its five to six centimeter reserve crown and root, lies with a concave bend to the mouth and almost parallel to the jaw. These teeth have no occlusion, meaning they have no contact with the opposing teeth.

The canines or tushes have lost their function as fighting teeth.

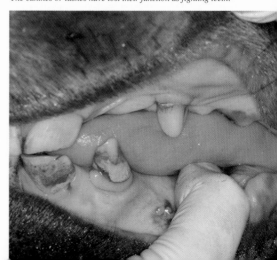

The canine does not erupt continuously as the other teeth. A problem often seen with the canine is a strong buildup of tartar, forming a ring around the bottom of the visible crown of the tooth. The opening of the salivary gland of the lower jaw is immediately next to the canine tooth. It has been said that the flow of saliva stimulates the buildup of limescale on the canines.

The wolf tooth

A small pointed tooth often develops just in front of the first functional cheek tooth. This little tooth is called the wolf tooth. This is a residual tooth that often has no length in its root. To this day this tooth can be found in zebras and wild horses as a fully functional tooth. In the domesticated horse, however, it is only anchored in the gum or has a thin bony connection to the jawbone. It is virtually always found in the top jaw, directly in front of the first premolar. Occasionally the wolf tooth is more to the front of the mouth, slightly in the direction of the tongue. In this position it can come into contact with the bit and can impair the control of the rider. The tongue and lips of the horse can be damaged or inflamed by these small pointed teeth, removal of which is perfectly simple. Occasionally they are grown into the upper jawbone with their roots and are broken off with extraction. This situation will seldom be attended by complications, however. From time to time the wolf teeth will stay beneath the surface of the gum. They are then called "blind," or unerupted, wolf teeth. They are irritated by the bit on the jaw and often cause unexplained trouble when the horse is being ridden.

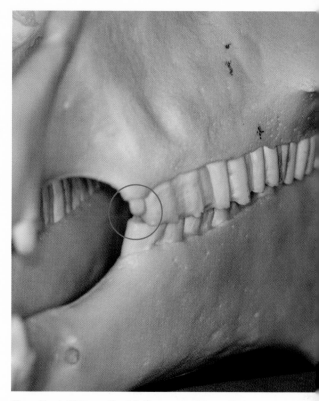

The wolf tooth (P1) is considered the first premolar. It is a residual tooth and has a small root.

By using finger pressure in this area, one can make a diagnosis on suspicion. The presence of a hidden wolf tooth can be confirmed with the use of radiographs.

Premolars and molars

The first three cheek teeth (premolars) are present as milk teeth as well. They are present at birth or will develop within the first week after birth. Unlike the deciduous incisors, the primary cheek teeth are of equal size, but show a narrowing at the transition from crown to root.

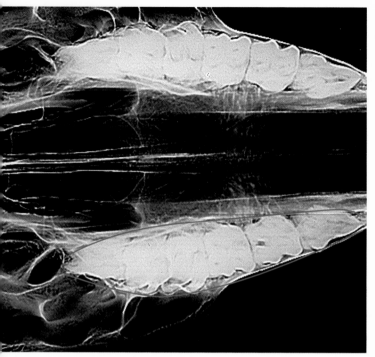

The chewing surfaces of the molars in the upper jaw taper to the front and the back.

top and bottom, giving each jaw a specific and interlocking chewing surface. The cheek teeth of the upper jaw are almost square and are wider than the teeth in the lower jaw. The first and last cheek teeth taper towards the ends of the chewing surface.

The cheek teeth of the lower jaw are more rectangular in shape and narrower than the teeth in the upper jaw. The lower cheek teeth also taper towards the ends of the chewing surface. The teeth run horizontally on a level plateau up to the last molar (M3). At the back there is a slight upwards curve, corresponding to the natural line of the bone in the lower jaw. This upward slope of the lower jaw varies according to the breed of the horse and the length of the head. In Arabian horses that naturally have shorter heads, the incline starts as far forward as the first molar (M1).

At the age of two and a half years, the first, at three years the second and at four years the third premolar is shed. The milk teeth will be pushed out from below by the permanent teeth. The rest of the root will be absorbed from the basis. A thin plate, the rest of the milk tooth, will remain on top of the new tooth. This plate is also called a cap.

The three back cheek teeth, the molars, have no milk teeth and appear as permanent teeth only. They erupt at one year of age for the first molar, at two years for the second molar and at three years for the third molar. The adult horse has a complete set of 24 cheek teeth at four years of age, six on each side,

The edges of the upper molars are smoother on the inside of the mouth. Ramps on the cheek side can cause serious trauma to the inside of the cheeks.

The surface area of the upper molars is irregularly bumpy, as on a rasp. There are two depots filled with cement on the molars of the upper jaw.

The Latin name for these depots is *infundibulum*. The teeth of the lower jaw have only one infundibulum per tooth. The borders of the molars are smoother on the inside of the mouth than on the side of the cheeks.

Molars, as with the incisors, only rise out of the gum a little. The visible crown is merely one to one and a half centimeters long. The rest of the crown embedded in the socket is up to seven centimeters long in a seven to eight-year-old horse. This makes the total length of the crown about eight centimeters. The crown gets ground down and erupts continuously throughout the life of the horse. The tooth gets worn away at roughly two to three millimeters per year, depending on the nourishment of the horse. When you think that a horse's teeth are in occlusion (biting on each other) at five years, it is safe to say that the teeth will be worn out completely at the age of 30 to 35. The first cheek tooth has a shorter reserve crown in the socket, which means this tooth will be worn out first. The upper molars have three roots, whereas the teeth in the lower jaw have only two.

The molars more to the front of the mouth are slightly slanted rearwards. This means that the root of the tooth points to the front a little and the crown leans to the back a bit. The last molar, in both the upper and lower jaws, goes against that by leaning in the opposite direction. In this way the first and last teeth actually press the intermediate teeth together. This construction is supported by the teeth in between the first and last teeth through their position in the jaw. The advantage of this is an extremely stable chewing surface that can withstand enormous pressure between the two jaws. The tight fit of the teeth against each other means that no food particles can get caught between them. This reduces the risk of injury or infection in the sockets.

The molar teeth are made of three substances: cement, dentine and enamel. The molars of the upper

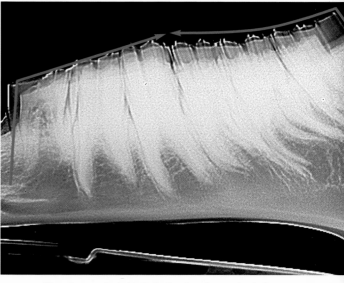

The molars are attached to the jawbone in such a way that the first and last molars actually push the others together. This has a marked stabilizing effect on the chewing surface.

jaw comprise type 1 enamel. Type 1 enamel is harder than type 2 enamel, found in the molars of the lower jaw and the incisors. The particular hardness of type 1 enamel can often lead to fractures of the molars in the upper jaw, while the lower molars with the softer type 2 enamel are more prone to faster wear, losing tooth substance unevenly as well.

Designation of the teeth with the tooth formula

The teeth of the horse are described as follows in older literature:		
Incisors	*Latin* Incisivus	*hence the letter "I"*
Central	*Tooth on midline*	*I1*
Intermediate	*Middle incisor*	*I2*
Corner	*Last incisor*	*I3*
Canine	*Latin* Caninus	*hence the letter "C"*
Premolars	*Latin* Praemolar	*hence the letter "P"*
Wolf tooth	*Tooth in front of the first real molar*	*P1*
1st to 3rd premolar		*P2-P4*
Molars	*Latin* Molar	*Hence the letter "M"*
1st to 3rd molar		*M1-M3*

Skull with color – coded tooth groups

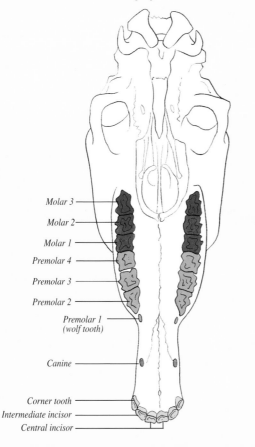

Molar 3
Molar 2
Molar 1
Premolar 4
Premolar 3
Premolar 2
Premolar 1 (wolf tooth)
Canine
Corner tooth
Intermediate incisor
Central incisor

This formula gives no indication whether the teeth are in the upper or lower jaw. To clarify the exact position of human teeth, there is a numbering system that gives each tooth a number. This system, called the Triadan system, is now used in veterinary medicine as well.

The Triadan numbering runs in the sequence upper right – upper left – lower left – lower right. The first designator refers to the quadrant of the jaw:

- upper right: 1
- upper left: 2
- lower left: 3
- lower right: 4

In order to distinguish them from the permanent teeth, the deciduous teeth are numbered:

- upper right: 5
- upper left: 6
- lower left: 7
- lower right: 8

Lower jaw

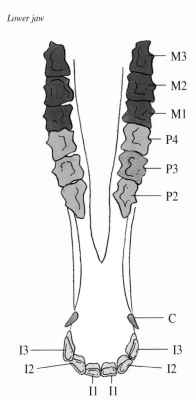

M3
M2
M1
P4
P3
P2

C

I3 — I3
I2 — I2
I1 I1

Upper jaw

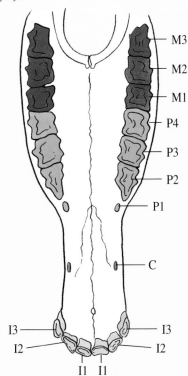

M3
M2
M1
P4
P3
P2
P1

C

I3 — I3
I2 — I2
I1 I1

The tooth formula and numbering of the teeth

After the quadrant number comes the number of the tooth. The incisors are numbered from the middle, 01 – 02 – 03. Hence the central incisor upper right is designated:

1 for the jaw position and 01 for the tooth, which gives 101.

The canine is numbered 04.

The canine lower right is then 404.

The wolf tooth is numbered 05.

The wolf tooth upper left is then 205.

The premolars are numbered 06 – 07 – 08, and the molars 09 – 10 – 11.

How does a tooth grow?

The different phases of tooth growth can be summarized as follows:

Step 1: Preparatory phase

The tooth bud lies in the jawbone. A fibrous capsule surrounding it guides the bud towards the gum.

Step 2: Young growth

The tooth continues to grow under the gum. The different tooth substances have already been formed.

Step 3: Eruption of the tooth through the gum

The tooth reaches the niveau of the gum, bulges the gum into the mouth and the tooth erupts.

Step 4: First contact with the opposing tooth

The erupted tooth reaches the niveau of the chewing surface and comes into contact with the opposing tooth

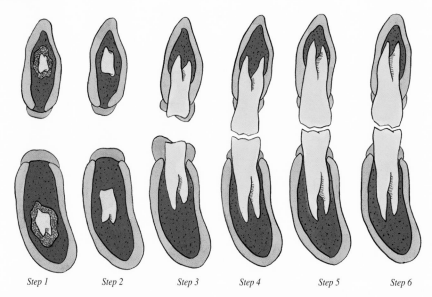

| Step 1 | Step 2 | Step 3 | Step 4 | Step 5 | Step 6 |

Development and growth of the teeth

for the first time. The young tooth is still covered by a layer of cementum.

Step 5: Tooth in occlusion (grinding against opposing tooth)

The tooth is grinding against the opposing tooth, fulfilling its task of crushing food into smaller particles.

Step 6: Tooth formation and eruption of the reserve crown

Tooth substance is produced until the horse is seven or eight years old. Thereafter the rest of the crown will keep on erupting in the mouth of the horse.

The role of the teeth in feeding

Incisors

The incisors of the horse are fully functional. Unlike ruminants, the horse has six stable front teeth in both the upper and lower jaw. In cattle there are no teeth in the upper jaw at the front and that space is a hardened chewing surface covered in gum. The advantage ruminants have over the horse is that they have a special digestive mechanism to ruminate, and absorb their food more efficiently this way. Horses, however, can cut off short grass and even pull out roots with their incisor teeth. The short grasses and roots contain the highest energy content of the whole plant. This makes it possible for the horse to survive hard and sparse conditions. This is not necessarily a good thing for horse owners, for paddocks can be ruined when horses unearth the grass on a constant basis.

Molars

The upper jaw of the horse is obviously wider than the lower jaw.

This means that the teeth from the two jaws do not lie exactly opposite each other. The teeth of the upper jaw overlap for only one third of their chewing surface the teeth of the lower jaw. The circular chewing motion of the lower jaw in contact with the upper jaw actively grinds the molars of the lower jaw against the passive upper jaw. This results in an extremely effective crushing of food particles, leading to successful digestion of food that would normally be hard or impossible to digest. The chewing surfaces of the molars have an angle of 10-15 degrees. The circular chewing motion of the lower jaw contributes to the enlargement of the chewing surface at this angle. All of these factors make the crushing of food exceptionally effective.

Determining age – How old is the horse?

How old is my horse?

Further digestion

The movement of the tongue then pushes the crushed food via the larynx into the gullet and the stomach of the horse, where digestion takes place. Acids in the stomach will then help to dissolve the food particles. The stomach of the horse is relatively small, and food rapidly gets transported further down to the small intestines. Saliva, stomach acids and further digestive enzymes will aid the mushy food in travelling to the caecum. Bacteria of various types will further the breakdown of starch in the caecum. The energy molecules from the food are now small enough to pass through the walls of the intestine and be absorbed by the body. The rest of the contents are dehydrated and passed out. Proper crushing of the food by the teeth and a proficient jaw is an important precondition for the process of digestion.

Second dentition

Determining the age of a horse has traditionally always been done with the help of the teeth. Eruption of the milk teeth and then the permanent teeth (second dentition), grating down of the cup in the incisors and the form and position of the teeth are indications of the age of a horse. In earlier days this was of great significance. Today most horses have a passport and can easily be identified with freeze brands and microchips. Nevertheless, determining age with dentition still plays an important role. The degree to which the horse's teeth have been ground down depends on various factors: how the horse is kept, the food it gets, position of the teeth and vices like cribbing will all influence the way the incisors are worn down. At one time, unscrupulous dealers used adventurous techniques for preparing horses' teeth to disguise their true age. Interestingly, horses always became younger rather than older.

Back to the present. As a rule of thumb one can say: the younger the horse, the better the possibility of determining its age accurately. The older the horse, the greater the influence of its lifestyle on the wear of the teeth. For this reason the age of the teeth do not necessarily mean the same as the age of the horse. Age determination is extremely easy when the secondary dentition erupts, chiefly with the incisors.

Newborn foals often have their central incisors, or will get them within a few days of birth. The intermediate incisors come through at four to six weeks and the corner incisors at six to nine months. As a rough calculation, one can say six days – six weeks – six months. This formula is easy to remember and helps to determine the age of foals. The crowns of the first incisors are shovel-shaped and end in a narrow stem at the roots. Milk teeth also have cups that get ground down and disappear after a while. In the central milk teeth the cup will disappear at twelve months; in the intermediate milk teeth it will vanish at 18 months; and in the corner milk teeth it will fade away at 24 months. Once the cup is completely ground away, the incisors will stop growing. The permanent incisors develop underneath the incisors of the milk teeth. They replace the milk teeth; the first to go are the central incisors at two and a half years, the intermediate incisors at three and a half years and the corner teeth at four and a half years. Each tooth needs approximately six months to reach the surface of occlusion. This means a horse with fully replaced and functional incisor dentition is five years old.

Canine teeth develop as milk teeth. They do not manage to break through the surface of the gum and are therefore not relevant to the determination of age.

The premolars are already present in the mouth at birth. They are replaced with permanent teeth at two and a half years for the first premolar, three years for the second premolar and three and a half to four years for the third premolar.

The molars are not present as deciduous teeth. They immediately erupt as permanent teeth at the age of one year for the first molar, two to two and a half years for the second molar and three and a half to four years for the third molar.

Assessing the deciduous dentition in ponies is frequently difficult. The incisors of the milk teeth are not as markedly different to the permanent incisors as is the case with horses. Ponies also look more grown up in terms of their bodily proportions than the foals of horses. A two-year-old pony has a deciduous incisor dentition that is hard to distinguish from a permanent incisor dentition. It normally is of assistance to look deeper into a pony's mouth. If the last molar has not yet erupted, the pony is probably two years old. If the last molar has erupted, it means that the permanent incisors are all present, and the pony must be at least five years old.

Age determination according to the wear on the chewing surfaces of the incisors

Aside from the eruption of the permanent incisors, the wear of the incisors is an important criterion of age determination in the adult horse after five years. The origin of the word "cup" has already been explained in this text. Cups are dentine-filled oval,

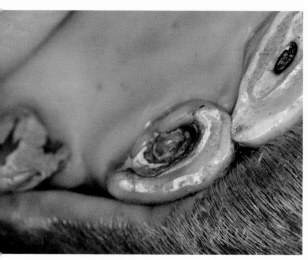

A cup in the corner incisor of the lower jaw.
It is roughly six millimeters deep.

take roughly six years to grind the cups away. Starting with the central incisors, the cups will be ground away at an age of nine years, on the intermediate incisors by the age of ten and on the corner incisors by the age of eleven.

The cups of the incisors in the upper jaw can have variable depths. Wear on them is not as constant as on the incisors of the lower jaw. Estimating the cups in the upper jaw is therefore not as reliable as the definition of the cups in the lower jaw.

black cavities on the chewing surface of the incisors, surrounded by enamel. The teeth in the lower jaw have cups that are on average six millimeters deep.

One calculates approximately two millimeters of wear per year. The cups of the central incisors in the lower jaw are completely ground away after three years. By three years of age the central incisors are in occlusion and start to wear. Three years later, at the age of six, the cups of the central incisors have been ground away. The horse's age according to the teeth is six. One can continue in this way. Worn away cups of the intermediate incisors mean that the horse is seven years old, while worn away cups of the corner incisors mean that the horse is eight years old. The only sign left of the original cup is a small dot instead of the cavity on the chewing surface, and this is known as the "mark."

The cups of the incisors in the upper jaw are about twelve millimetres deep. If one calculates a wear of two millimetres per year on these, it will

The cups of the lower incisors disappear at the age of six at the centrals, at seven at the intermediates and at eight at the corners.

6 years

7 years

8 years

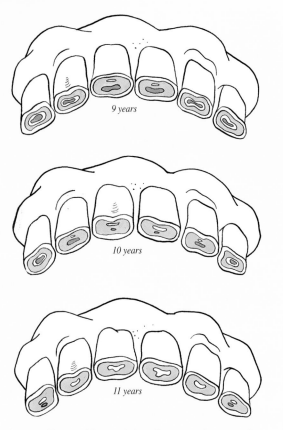

9 years

10 years

11 years

The cups of the upper incisors disappear at nine years at the centrals, at ten years at the intermediates and at eleven years at the corners.

Beside the cup, the dental star also appears from the age of six. This is a small, dark-to-light brown spot on the chewing surface of the incisors. The star is found in front of the cup, closer to the lips (see page 39 on anatomy). The dental star can be seen on the central incisors of the lower jaw at the age of six, at seven on the intermediate incisors and at eight on the corner incisors. The mani-

festation of the dental star in the incisors of the upper jaw is not reliable enough for the determination of age. Dental stars in the incisors of the upper jaw emerge much later than those in the lower jaw.

Shape of the chewing surfaces of the incisors

The shape of the chewing surface of the lower incisors changes with age. The young tooth is diagonally oval up to the age of twelve years. Between 13 and 18 it changes to a rounder form, and from 18 to 23 it is more triangular. From the age of 23 onwards, the shape is more vertically oval. This age determination is not very reliable, however, and can only be used as a supplementary tool.

Dental star and mark

The teeth get ground down with age. This means the image of the surface will change.

The dental star is the tooth pulp sealed with dentine (darker spot towards the front). The mark is the rest of the cup (darker spot towards the back).

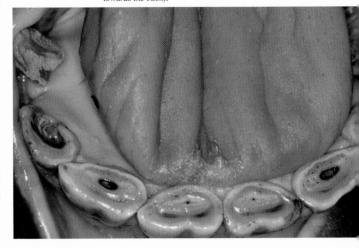

The cup is, as already discussed, ground down. The cup is surrounded with enamel.

Enamel is the hardest substance found in the body, and therefore it takes the longest to grind it down. The cup, that changes into the mark as it gets worn down, is slightly higher due to the enamel surrounding it.

Directly in front of the cup, the dental star becomes visible with age. In the centrals it starts to disappear at six, the intermediates at seven and the corners at eight. The mark recedes completely at thirteen, fourteen and fifteen years from the respective teeth. The dental star is the tooth pulp sealed with secondary dentine. With the eruption of the reserve crown, the pulp gets sealed with dentine from the inside out. The dental star stay for the rest of the horse's life, even when the mark disappears completely. The secondary dentine that represents the dental star is not as hard as enamel. The dental star will therefore not be as pronounced above the niveau of the chewing surface as the mark. If any borderline case exists, it is important to know the difference between the mark and the dental star (see fingernail test, page 22).

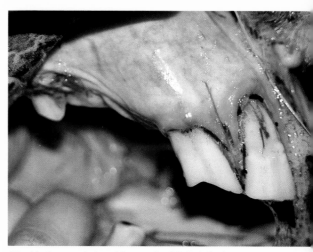

A hook in the corner incisor of the upper jaw. This hook develops at seven with the different development between the upper and lower jaws.

hook develops on the back half of the upper tooth that is not being ground down. This hook is formed at around nine to ten years. The upper teeth are then moved forward into a horizontal position at about twelve, and this hook disappears again. The same movement occurs at about 15 to 16 years, and a second hook forms. This second hook balances out at 18 years. Around 20 years of age a third hook can form that stays for a much longer time.

Hooks on the upper corner incisors

Another criterion for age determination is the so-called hooks. At approximately seven years of age, the position of the lower incisors changes. Their chewing surface moves and they extend to the front at a more horizontal angle. The surface of the upper corner incisor is then only 50 percent in contact (and occlusion) with the lower corner incisor. A sharp

The length-width proportion of the corner tooth in the upper jaw

A further indication of the age of the horse is the length-width proportion of the corner tooth in the upper jaw. A young corner tooth is wider where it meets the gum than it is long. The older the horse gets, the longer the visible crown in proportion to the width. At about ten years of age the visible crown is longer than it is wide at gum level.

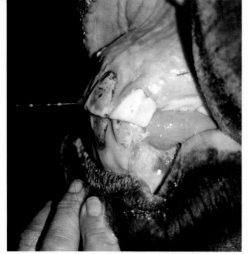

The length-width proportion of the visible crown of the upper corner incisor helps to determine age in a horse. Up to the tenth year, the base of the tooth is wider than it is long. The horse in the upper picture is six, while that in the bottom picture is twenty-eight.

The position of the incisors in relation to each other

The appearance in profile of the upper and lower arcades is always referred to by their angle, and the angle can be described as steep, protruding, acute, etc. In profile, the upper and lower arcades of a young horse are very close to a straight line from the gum of the upper arcade to the occlusal surfaces and down to the gum line of the lower arcade. As

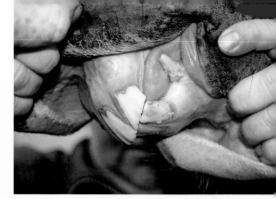

A young horse, six years old

A mature horse, twelve years old

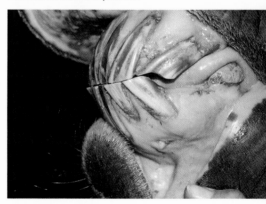

An old horse, twenty years old

A very old horse, older than thirty. Dentition of an old horse: the teeth are pointed almost horizontally to the front. This develops from a straight to an angular dentition.

aging occurs this angle becomes more acute (near 120 degrees or less), usually significantly so around 20 years of age. The lower arcade generally takes up the more oblique position.

The change in the angle of the teeth is based on the fact that they rest perpendicularly on each other up to the ninth year. The lower incisors move into an angle much quicker than the teeth of the upper jaw. From the age of fifteen the angle of the upper jaw catches up with the lower jaw, and the protrusion is started.

Grooves on the upper corner incisors

The outer surface of the upper corner incisors will start to develop a groove from the level of the gum at the age of ten. These are also called the grooves of Galvayne. At fifteen this groove is down at the halfway mark of the tooth. At twenty the groove is along the whole length of the tooth, right up to the chewing surface. On further eruption of the tooth, the groove will be visible only in the lower half of the tooth from the age of twenty-five. Horses older than thirty will have just the last bit of the groove visible at the chewing surface of the tooth.

> The groove on the side of the corner incisor provides ample information on the age of the horse. When the groove reaches the middle of the visible crown, the horse is roughly fifteen years old. (See photo.)

Age determination

Determining the age of a horse using the changes in dentition will only be approximately correct. As discussed earlier, external factors like feeding and how the horse is kept will influence the wear of the teeth. For example, horses kept on sandy soil will wear their incisors more rapidly.

There is more corrective dentistry undertaken in the modern horse from a medical point of view than ever before. This can change the evidence about the age of the teeth considerably.

The breed of the horse also plays a role in the determination of age. Ponies often mature late, and their dentition is delayed accordingly. One example is that the cups in the incisors of the lower jaw only disappear at nine to ten years. One should always remember to take this into account when trying to determine the age of ponies.

The groove of a 15-year-old horse

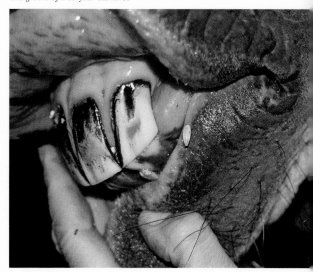

Overview of age determination in horse dentition

Birth to 6 days	Primary central incisors existing, primary molars existing
6 weeks	Primary intermediate incisors erupt
6 months	Primary corner incisors erupt
12 months	Cups in primary centrals disappear in lower jaw, M1 erupts
18 months	Cups in primary intermediates disappear in lower jaw
24 months	Cups in primary corner incisors disappear, M2 erupts
$2^1/_2$ years	Primary centrals shed, primary premolars P2 shed
3 years	Primary premolars P3 shed
$3^1/_2$ years	Primary intermediates shed
4 years	Primary premolars P4 shed
$4^1/_2$ years	Primary corner incisors shed
4-5 years	Canines erupt, M3 existing
6 years	Cups in the lower centrals disappear
7 years	Cups in the lower intermediates disappear
8 years	Cups in the lower corner incisors disappear, incisors perpendicular to each other
9 years	Cups in the upper centrals disappear
10 years	Cups in the upper intermediates disappear, groove develops on upper corner incisors at gum level, hooks on upper corner incisors, upper corner incisor longer than wide
11 years	Cups in the upper corner incisors disappear
12 years	Chewing surface of lower centrals becomes rounder, hooks on upper corner incisors disappear
13 years	Chewing surface of the lower intermediates becomes rounder, marks on the lower incisors disappear
14 years	Chewing surface of the lower corner incisors becomes rounder, marks on lower intermediates disappear
15 years	Marks on lower corner incisors disappear, second hook is formed on upper corner incisor, Galvayne groove in middle of upper corner incisor, lower incisors protrude further
18 years	Second hook on upper corner incisors disappears
20 years	Third hook forms on upper corner incisors, horizontal position of incisors in upper and lower jaw tables (chewing surfaces) has become triangular, Galvayne groove continuous through upper corner incisors
25 years	Galvayne groove only visible in lower half of tooth, chewing surfaces of the incisors are vertically oval
30 years	Galvayne groove only visible on lower part of the corner incisors, incisors extremely pointed to the front, teeth exceedingly long

Anatomy of the jaw and the position of the teeth in the jawbone

The jawbone is the bony foundation of the tooth. Over the period of the horse's evolution, the jawbone has developed a longer base with tremendous size. The reason is the need for more space for the teeth, these having changed as much themselves. The upper jaw is wider than the lower jaw.

The upper jaw forms a cohesive unit with the rest of the skull. The incisors, canines, wolf teeth (when present), the first and second premolars, and the front aspect of the third molars are all implanted in the bone of the upper jaw. In three- to five-year-old horses one can see a typical localized swelling in the position of the first three premolars and the molars. This swelling is typical in the formation phase of the teeth. A similar phenomenon is seen in the lower jaw. All the teeth are firmly implanted in the lower jaw. During the formation of the teeth, these localized swellings can occur. These swellings are also known as bumps. At the fifth to sixth year, these bumps will disappear altogether. The tooth substance has then been developed to a greater degree, and the permanent teeth are embedded in their final position in the jaw.

The last premolar and the first molar in the upper jaw lie in the front part of the maxillary sinus (maxilla=upper jaw). The last two molars both lie in the rear part of the maxillary sinus. No swelling develops here when the teeth are being formed. The tooth structure has enough available space to develop without spreading out into neighboring tissues. In exceptional cases the nasal cavity could be narrowed down through the bony changes that take place during the formation of the teeth. There is a relatively big sinus in the upper jaw. This is connected to the maxillary sinus, and they are both ventilated via the nasal passage.

The lower jaw is the largest bone in the skull. Unlike the frontal and maxillary sinuses in the upper jaw, there are no cavities in the bone of the lower jaw. The teeth of the lower jaw are all tightly implanted into the bone. The reaction to the production of teeth in the lower jaw can easily be seen in the area of the premolars and the first molar.

A view into the mouth of the horse. The lower jaw is narrower than the upper jaw. The 15-degree angle of the chewing surface on the molars is clearly visible.

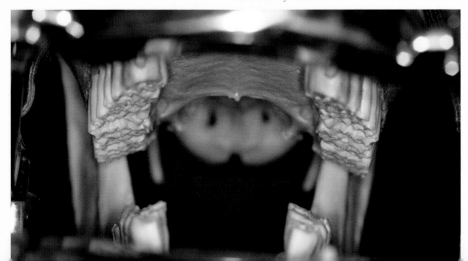

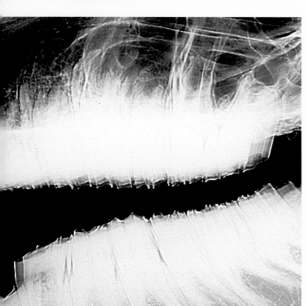

The jaws and their teeth

Only 30 percent of the chewing surface of the upper teeth (when resting) is covered by the teeth of the lower jaw. The flexibly jointed lower jaw is mobile and communicates with the upper jaw. The intrinsic tongue musculature stabilizes this movement. The joint of the jaw facilitates the horizontal opening of the mouth and allows additional sideways movement. The lower jaw can then maneuver around with circular movements on the wider, fixed upper jaw. The chewing surfaces of the teeth are at an angle of 10 to 15 degrees to each other. This, together with the strong chewing muscles, facilitates the optimal crushing of food particles.

What happens in and around the mouth of the horse?

The jaw joint

The jaw joint lies approximately 15 centimeters above the line where the molars meet. Looking at it on a live horse, it is five to six centimeters behind the back of the eye.

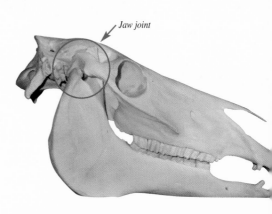

Position of the jaw joint

The arrangement is such that there is considerable leverage, together with the powerful chewing muscles. The joint also allows horizontal opening of the mouth and movement to the side, making it possible for the horse to grind the lower jaw against the upper jaw.

Salivary glands

There are three pairs of salivary glands in the horse, the biggest being the parotid salivary gland. This gland produces up to 50 milliliters of saliva per minute. The parotid salivary gland runs from the base of the ear beyond the lower jaw downwards, where it splits in two, one to the front and one to the back. The one to the front lies flanked by the branches of the blood vessels of the lower jawbone, and the one to the back lies in the base of the neck. In rider terms this is called the jowl of the horse. A constricted space between the bones of the lower jaw and an obvious parotid gland is considered limited jowl space. The duct of the parotid gland proceeds on the inside of the lower jaw until it joins up with the blood vessels on the lower edge of the jaw to advance further forward on the outer side of the jawbone. At the approximate area of P4, the salivary duct opens into the mouth of the horse. The parotid gland plays an important role in the ridden horse. A noseband will put pressure on the duct of the parotid gland. This pressure will restrict the secretion of saliva to the mouth. This will stimulate the horse to chew on the bit, and one will often see foam escaping from the mouth of the horse. In literature this is considered a sign of acceptance of

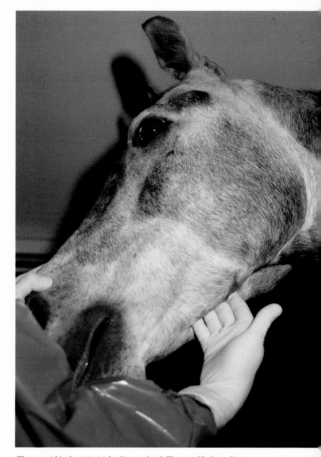

The parotid is the principal salivary gland. The mandibular salivary gland lies between the bones of the lower jaw towards the back, and the sublingual gland lies more to the front.

the bit and lightness, more specific in the dressage horse. This is not the complete truth. Even horses that are forced into an outline will salivate, for the same pressure will be exerted on their salivary ducts. The production of saliva does not necessarily have anything to do with the rideability of the horse. Anatomical proportions such as the width of the lower jaw and the size of the parotid gland are the decisive factors in the amount of saliva excreted.

The second largest salivary gland is the mandibular gland (*mandibula*=lower jaw).

This gland lies between the bones of the lower jaw. The duct of the mandibular gland opens in the mouth in the area of the canine teeth. The parotid and mandibular salivary glands are integrated with the lymph nodes of the lymphatic system. This construction means that the glands sometimes swell up in the spring and when the animals are out at pasture. The lymphatic system is incredibly sensitive to the blooms of grass and herbs.

The third and smallest salivary gland is the sublingual gland. This gland is to the front of the jawbone, under the tongue. The duct ends in numerous little openings in this area. There are various additional saliva producing glands to be found in the lips, tongue, gums and the mucous membrane of the mouth.

Swelling can sometimes, although seldom, be caused by stones in the salivary gland.

The tongue

The tongue of the horse is very big and completely fills the space between the teeth. Hooks and ramps on the teeth will therefore soon irritate the tongue.

The tongue is mainly made up of muscle. It is covered with a mucous membrane that has an enduring quality and is even calloused in places. The tongue has a bone (the hyoid bone) that stabilizes it at the base. This bone is mobile and is attached by muscles to the bone of the upper jaw. It is remarkably thin and can easily be damaged by awkward objects. The tongue is fixed to the lower jaw via the frenulum. The tongue moves

with the help of the long tongue muscles. These muscles extend from the back of the tongue over the lower neck to the junction of the torso. These muscles move the tongue and influence the mechanics of the lower jaw. The opening of the lower jaw when the horse chews depends greatly on the long muscles of the tongue.

Muscles of the mouth

The main chewing muscle is the cheek muscle, in Latin the *Masseter*. The chewing muscles of the horse are highly developed and not only open and close the lower jaw, but also move it sideways. This characteristic, together with the flexible jaw joint, makes it possible for the horse to grind tough food so well, that it elevates the nutritional value even of foodstuff that is normally difficult to digest.

The long tongue muscle opens the mouth. This is not an act of immense power, for gravity supports

The highly sensitive top lip selects and takes the food in.

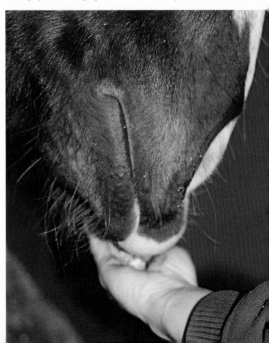

this opening up, meaning the muscle only has a subordinate function.

The more important muscle is the tongue itself. The horse has a large, long tongue that is almost exclusively made up of muscle.

The lips of the horse are highly mobile, well muscled and incredibly sensitive. The top lip has many groups of muscles that operate together in an exceptional way, which can be seen when the horse very carefully picks a treat from a hand. The sensitivity and mobility of the top lip is tremendously impressive to observe. The top lip will basically select the food the horse eats. The superb musculature and the perceptive mucous membrane of the lip guarantee the selective ingestion of wholesome food.

The mucous membrane

The mucous membrane of the top lip is highly receptive and can even perceive smells through particular receptors. These receptors are intensely used in the Flehmen response.

The mucous membrane of the mouth is of a particularly tough composition and is partly hardened. A big part of the mucous membrane of the mouth is grown into the underlying bone. The mucous membrane of the hard palate that forms the roof of the mouth has many wedge-shaped horizontal ridges that help to prevent food from dropping out of the mouth. There are 18 pairs of half-moon shaped ridges that meet in the center of the palate.

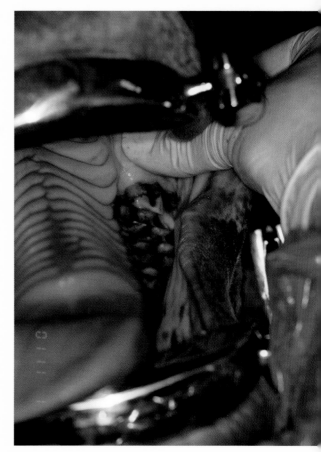

The palate of the horse has wedge-shaped horizontal ridges that help to prevent food from falling out of the mouth.

The nasal cavities

The frontal and maxillary sinuses are classified as nasal cavities. The head of the horse has grown longer as the requirements for more space for the teeth grew.

The weight of the skull is relatively small in relation to its size, due to the large empty spaces. The maxillary sinuses are equal on both sides and are the same size. The nasal septum separates the skull in two halves. The molars of the upper jaw jut into the maxillary sinuses and take up almost all of the space inside. The teeth continually erupt into the mouth throughout the life of the horse. In old horses these jaw cavities are filled with air instead of teeth. The teeth are obviously heavier than the air and this suggests that the skull of an old horse is considerably lighter than that of a seven or eight-year-old horse.

The maxillary sinus is subdivided into front and rear halves. The front part borders forward on the P3 and backwards at the M1. Directly behind that the rear part of the sinus starts, ending around the region of the M3. A thin bony wall with only a tiny hole that links them separates the two parts. At roughly the height of this little hole is where the mutual exit lies to the nasal cavity. The nasal cavity leads to the nostrils, creating a connection to the outside. This also makes possible the ventilation of the nasal cavity.

The frontal sinuses are between the eyes in the area of the forehead and are connected to the rear part of the maxillary sinuses. The teeth do not jut into these sinuses.

The nasolacrimal duct

The nasolacrimal (*naso*=nose, *lacrima*=tear) duct travels from the inner corner of the eye on the inside of the jaw to the roof of the maxillary sinus. From here it continues over the front of the jaw maxillary

sinus, integrates with the bone of the jaw and leaves the bone again in the region of the nostrils. Inflammation of the nasolacrimal duct is often caused by a tooth or jaw cavity infection.

Nervous supply to the mouth

All the teeth of the upper jaw are supplied by one nerve. This nerve exits through a small opening in the bones of the upper jaw. This opening is called the *Foramen infraorbitale* in Latin (= opening below the eye). This opening is relatively easy to

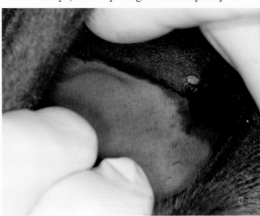

The nasolacrimal duct commences under the eye, runs above the maxillary sinus and ends near the nostrils. It is easy to irrigate it from here.

palpate. It can be found slightly above the line made between the front portion of the facial crest and the hind section of the bony angle of the nose. An injection of a local anaesthetic to this site can ensure pain-free treatment of the molars, canine and incisors of the upper jaw on that specific side.

The incisors, canine and premolars of the lower jaw can equally be influenced by a localized elimination of pain.

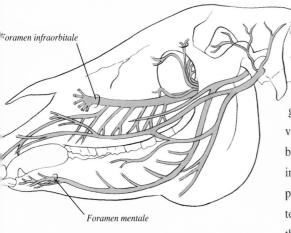

Foramen infraorbitale

Foramen mentale

The nervous supply to the head

The opening of the nerve to the lower jaw, the *Foramen mentale*, is approximately two fingers' breadth behind and below the corner of the mouth. A curb chain of a double bridle or Pelham that is too far to the back, can act as a stimulant to the nerve and report pain from this area.

The molars of the lower jaw can be blocked via the main nerve to the lower jaw. This nerve, however, lies very deep between the branches of the lower jaw and is not easy to localize. The need to eliminate pain in the molars of the lower jaw is not often demanded. When the need for a major intervention arises, or if the molars must be extracted, it is recommended to give the horse a general anesthetic.

The facial nerve that supplies the superficial structures of the head in the areas of the mouth is itself extremely superficial and can easily be damaged. A blow or kick to the nerve, which lies on the line of the molars, can lead to temporary or even permanent damage of the function of the nerve. Paralysis of the lips and sides of the face can result.

Blood vessels of the mouth

The mouth is intensely supplied with blood vessels. The mucous membranes of the cheeks, gums and lips are endowed with branched blood vessels, and the mucous membrane will easily bleed, even when only lightly injured. There are two important blood vessels that run on each side of the palate. These blood vessels have greater meaning to anyone examining the mouth of the horse, for they bleed profusely when injured. Placing a sharp mouth speculum in the mouth or improper use of the tooth rasp or other instruments can easily lead to damage of the palate and the blood vessels.

Once the blood mixes with saliva, it can be a dramatic sight. This situation is not necessarily life-threatening, however.

Blood vessels to the head of the horse

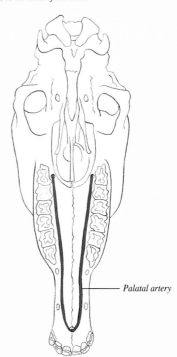

Palatal artery

How food is chewed

The head of the horse is essentially a tool for the intake and grinding of food. The mouth can be considered a grinding machine, with the teeth as millstones. These millstones are embedded in the jawbones, and in the area where the molars are implanted, they form a unit in the shape of a functional chewing surface. The jaw joints are the mobile units. They make the grinding of the food possible. The sensitive lips carefully select food and then work it in the direction of the incisors. The incisors cut short grass and roots and continue the supply until the mouth is filled. Only when enough food is in the mouth can the tongue, cheeks and ridges of the palate move it in the direction of the molars. The chewing muscles operate to grind the food into smaller particles by actively moving the jaw and teeth against each other and at the same time opening the mouth for more food. Once the food is sufficiently ground down, it gets transported to the gullet (esophagus).

The sideways movement in the grinding phase brings the narrower lower jaw into contact with the wider upper jaw. The strength of the muscle is increased by the buildup of pressure at the side where the lower jaw is pushed, and the teeth are then moved back across each other. The 10-15 degree slant of the molars means that the incisors will slightly lift away from each other during the chewing phase. In the second part of the chewing phase, the force is moved across the molars.

The operation of this mechanism is indicated by the evenness with which the teeth tend to be ground down. Horses have a tendency to favor one direction

The chewing movement of the horse has four phases:

Phase one is the opening of the mouth that requires little energy and is almost passively performed by gravity.
Phase two uses moderate energy to close the mouth.
Phase three is the actual working phase where the two jaws are pressed upon each other and moved sideways across each other.
The fourth phase is the relaxation phase, and from here the jaw goes back to the first phase.

of chewing. Notwithstanding the mechanism described above, there are many horses whose teeth wear unevenly. Unevenness of the wearing should be recognized and treated accordingly in the routine dental examinations.

In mass screening it was established that only 10 percent of horses use both the left and right sides of the jaw equally when chewing. The other 90 percent preferred one side to the other and revealed uneven wear of the surfaces.

The mechanics of chewing, together with the movement of the tongue and the ridges on the palate, transfer the food slowly to the back of the mouth. The construction of the palate, as already described, will prevent food from tumbling out.

The consistency of the food also has an influence on the intensity of the sideways movement. When the food is dry, the grinding movement of the lower jaw is less pronounced.

Figures about chewing

- Single ingested measure – a mouthful:
  10 grams of food
- Number of times the horse chews
  in a minute: 60-70
- Occurrence of grinding before the
  horse chews: 0.5-0.6 seconds
- Maximum displacement of the incisors:
  4-4.5 cm
- Displacement of the jaw before
  the molars touch: width of half an incisor

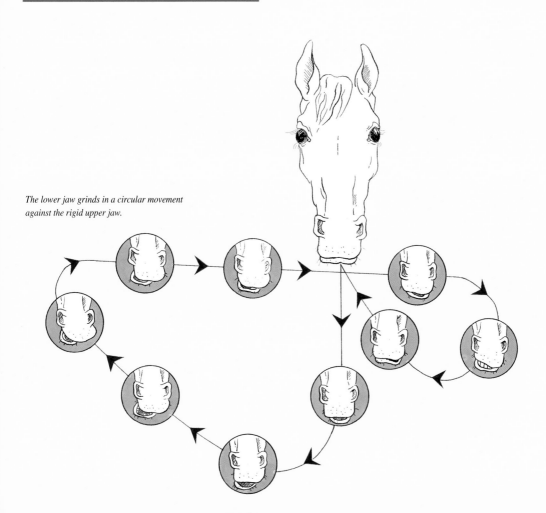

The lower jaw grinds in a circular movement
against the rigid upper jaw.

Diseases of the Teeth and Mouth

4

Diseases of the teeth

The mouth and teeth of horses are often poorly cared for. Horses that cannot ingest or chew their food properly are unable to perform well. The smallest pain in the mouth will influence the character of a horse. Back problems, fighting the bit, throwing the head, leaning on the rein and many

Horse with toothache

more problems are often connected with the teeth. The rideability of the horse is reduced, as is its athletic ability and the general enjoyment of riding it. Small problems in the mouth often cause big complications elsewhere. Oral and dental problems are generally easy to solve once you know what the problem is. The most important illnesses and their symptoms are summarized in this chapter to simplify the diagnosis of the problems surrounding the mouth and teeth.

Ramps and hooks on the molars

The chewing surfaces of the molars do not cover each other completely. The upper jaw is wider than the lower jaw. The molars of the lower jaw grind against the molars of the rigid upper jaw. To counteract the grinding down of the teeth, they continue to erupt over the horse's lifetime.

When the horse does not grind the food properly, bundles will form in the cheeks and fall out of the mouth (quidding). It is a sure sign of problems with the teeth when these bundles of food are found on the floor or in the manger.

It will frequently happen that the teeth are not worn as fast as they erupt. Uneven lengths of teeth will then appear as a result. These different lengths are called hooks or ramps, depending on their shapes and where they are formed. This is the most common problem when the horse cannot eat properly.

The projecting rest of the first or last molar that has not been worn down is considered a hook. These hooks have nothing in common with the canine teeth, also called stallion teeth, that grow in the space between the incisors and the molars.

The lower jaw is set back a little in a lot of horses. This is easiest to recognize at the incisors where the incisors of the lower jaw are slightly displaced to the back.

The lower jaw of the older horse is often set back a little. This causes the upper premolar (P2) to be out of the area of wear.

The rows of molars in the upper and lower jaw are of equal length. Correspondingly, the last tooth (M3) in the lower jaw will have a hook. The hook on P2 of the upper jaw can be extremely sharp and can injure the tongue and lips when the horse chews. This can lead to chronic injury with understandable pain accompanying it. Horses with this problem will only bite food and will not grind it any more. The dietary utilization of the food is reduced, and the condition of the horse will gradually deteriorate. Riding these horses causes problems as well. The bit will put pressure on the tongue. The horse will try to avoid this by moving the tongue to the front and back but also to the side. This friction on the tongue will cause even more trauma and the horse will evade the bit.

Floating the hook on the P2 will temporarily solve the problem. The infection on the tongue will heal within two to three days, and the horse will be free of symptoms.

Hooks on the M3, the last molar on the lower jaw, are more difficult to detect. The formation of the hook on M3 almost always forms in connection with the hook on P2. These horses will often shake their heads when ridden and will be poor feeders. In this case the mucous membrane of the

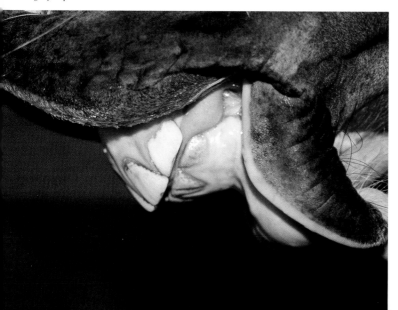

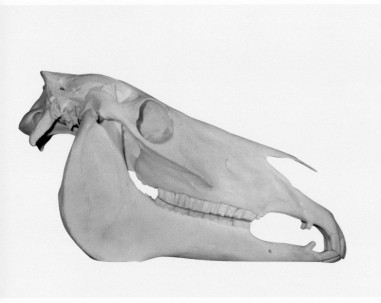

The chewing surface of the molars curves upwards towards the back. Seeing the back teeth and the treatment of the back teeth is made difficult because of this.

can be made extremely uncomfortable through too tight nosebands, and the horse will try to fight against the constraint. Head-shaking, fighting against the bit and even rearing when the reins are taken up are the most common symptoms. Recognizing this problem is difficult because the last tooth is not easy to examine. (See page 87ff. – how the examination of teeth and mouth is carried out.) The treatment, the floating of the tooth, is even more difficult, for the last tooth is deep to the back of the mouth where it is hard to see.

opposite upper jaw will be stimulated and chewing will be painful.

In horses with shorter heads, for example the Arabians, the last two molars, M2 and M3, lie on the upward curve of the lower jaw. The chewing surface of the lower jaw runs in a more or less steep curve to the top.

A hook on the last molar of the lower jaw, together with the anatomical construction of the jaw, can have extreme consequences with regard to the temperament of the ridden horse. The ridden horse curves its neck, the poll becoming the highest point, and the nasal bone moves into a vertical position. This position of the head causes the lower jaw to move slightly to the front of the upper jaw. If there are hooks, this gliding mechanism cannot operate. Tension develops between the two jaws, and pressure on the jaw joints is increased. This pressure

The anatomical construction of the curving lower jaw has to be followed when floating the teeth. If the hook on the last tooth of the lower jaw is really big, the large last molar of the upper jaw will partially obscure it. The mouth has to be opened extremely wide for the optimum treatment of this problem. This is the only way to float the hook on the tooth. Extremely big hooks on the M3 must sometimes be treated under general anesthesia.

Projections on the sides of teeth are classified as ramps. From a certain age, almost all horses will have ramps on the molars of both the upper and lower jaws. This is the result of inadequate chewing and thus inadequate grinding down of the teeth. The lower jaw grinds against the upper jaw. In the resting phase the opposing jaw only covers about 30 percent of the chewing surface. During the active chewing phase the teeth of the lower jaw must grind down the total surface of the teeth of the upper jaw.

To achieve this the lower jaw moves in gentle circles against the upper jaw. This results in a chewing surface with a 10-15 degree angle. If the intensity of chewing is insufficient, the chewing circle will not be completed to the outer edges of the molars on the upper jaw. In this way sharp banks will come into being on the outer surfaces of the upper molars. These ramps on the upper molars will irritate the mucous membrane of the cheeks. The chewing intensity is then decreased even more due to the pain of the cheeks, making the ramps bigger, and the situation worsens.

The lower jaw is narrower than the upper jaw, as are the chewing surfaces of the molars. For this reason one will seldom find any ramps on the molars of the lower jaw, although in horses that have acutely narrow lower jaws, or where the chewing action is greatly diminished, one will sometimes find ramps on the molars of the lower jaw. These ramps, however, are on the inside edges of the teeth. Small, sharp ramps in this area will quickly injure the tongue.

The tongue of the horse is immensely mobile and responsible for the further transport of the ingested food. Considering the length and size of the horse's mouth, the task of the tongue should not be underestimated.

In a closed mouth the tongue fills the whole space between the teeth. Negative stimulus of the tongue will seriously influence the activ-

ity of the tongue. Food will not be transferred further down the mouth. The chewing movement will be trivialized, as any movement of the jaw will aggravate the inflamed tongue even more. Instead of then grinding and moving the food from the space between the jaws, there will be a build-up of food between the teeth and the cheeks. The horse bites on the food as if on chewing gum. The food is wrapped around itself and these balls, mainly hay or grass, will fall from the horse's mouth. When this happens, it is a sure sign of hooks or ramps. The poor chewing and the unsatisfactory chopping of food can also lead to blockage of the gullet. In this case the level of the molars should also be inspected.

The sharp sides of the molars must then be floated. The 10-15 degree angle should be retained to ensure optimum activity. In earlier times, a highly rounded profile would have been the outcome.

Sharp ramps on the sides of the molars can be floated.
In this photo the sharp ramps can easily be seen on the insides
of the lower molars.

Nowadays we know that this decreases the chewing surface and damages the tooth substance. When floating the teeth, the horizontal surface must be balanced and the ramps rounded.

Further irregular wear of the molars

An extreme inclination of the chewing surface of the molars of 20 degrees or more is not effective. This is called a "shear mouth." This faulty angle of the chewing surface develops in horses with an extremely narrow lower jaw. With the passing of time the correct chewing motion diminishes in view of the fact that the lower jaw can only be used against the upper jaw under extreme pressure. The result is the development of ramps on the outside edge of the upper molars and on the inside edge of the lower molars. In circumstances like this, the normal chewing surface angle of 10-15 degrees must be achieved through regular floating.

Aside from the development of hooks and ramps on the molars, the chewing capacity can also be influenced by the irregular wear of single teeth. If a tooth is missing in the chewing surface, this means that the opposing tooth will not be ground down and will continue to erupt. A tooth that develops in this way is often called a chisel mouth. After a while this over-erupting tooth will bite so deep into the space on the opposite side that it will squash onto the gum that covers that space. This in turn will lead to inflammation and in extreme cases even damage to the jawbone. At this stage a gliding, even movement of the lower jaw from side to side and forwards and backwards is no longer possible. The

result is that hooks and ramps develop as well as the above-mentioned problem. Regular floating of the erupting tooth can solve this problem. A regular twice yearly examination is recommended.

Older horses often have irregular wear in a whole row of molars. To the front of the mouth, molars of the upper jaw are worn more rapidly than the opposing molars in the lower jaw. Towards the back of the mouth the opposite is true. In the course of time this will form a vicious circle. The unrelenting rise of pressure from the longer teeth against the already heavily worn opposing teeth will lead to a state of continual discrepancy. If this situation is not treated early, it can lead to premature loss of teeth. The treatment of this problem is the floating of the longer teeth. If teeth are exceptionally long, they should not be shortened to the optimum length in one go. On the one hand, the extreme shortening of the teeth could expose the tooth pulp, and this will surely lead to an infection. On the other hand, the jaw joint must also get used to the new situation. When this is done in stages, it will be easier for the jaw to adapt.

The wave mouth, seen from the side, will show, as the name suggests, a wave in its course. It is often the first molars of the lower jaw that are longer than in the upper jaw. The niveau descends in the region of P3/P4, only to rise again around M1. In the area of the M2, it runs into a valley again and rises up to end in a hill at M3. The situation in the upper jaw is correspondingly the opposite.

The chewing mechanics and the smooth gliding movement of the molars against each other in this case is obviously impossible. Floating the hilly parts of the wave is the solution to the problem.

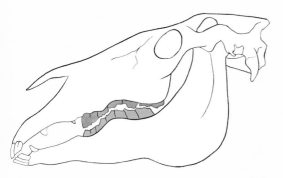

A curved, irregular chewing surface on the molars is called a wave mouth

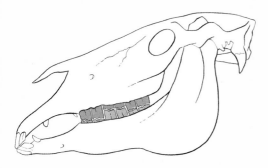

A terraced irregular chewing surface on the molars is called a step mouth.

Irregular wear of the incisors

Not only is there wear on the molars, but it is also apparent on the incisors. The incisors are only seldom taken into consideration when examining the mouth. Problems here, however, can have the same repercussions on the chewing activity and the temperament of the ridden horse as with the molars.

If an incisor is absent, the tooth opposite will grow into the space. Irritation of the gum and the jawbone is the result. The over-erupted tooth will inhibit the sideways movement of the lower jaw against the upper jaw. The grinding effect is blocked, the chopping up of the food prevented and the digestion of the food reduced. Power tools can be used to shorten the tooth to the level of the others. If the tooth is very long, this should be done in stages, or the danger of opening the pulp will be imminent.

Irregular chewing on one side of the mouth only will add to the uneven wear of the incisors. When looking at the incisors from the front, one will notice

The terraced look when viewed from the side is called a step mouth. In most cases a step is visible between the last premolar and the first molar. Floating of the step defect, when necessary in more than one attempt, will balance the chewing surface once more.

The incisors of this horse are not of equal length. The wear is one-sided.

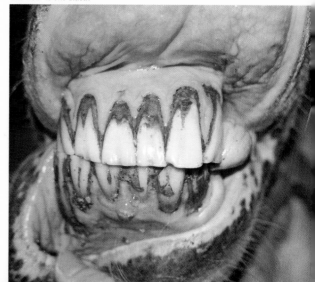

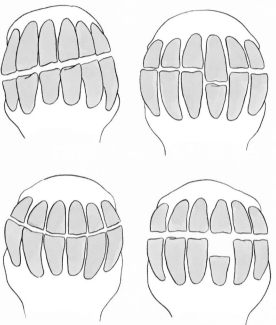

Irregular wear of the incisors seen from the front

insufficiently. They end up being too long, while the molars are worn down through the chewing motion. In time the over-long incisors will prevent the molars from touching. Food will not be properly chopped up. Reducing the length of the incisors in the upper and lower jaw to a niveau where the molars touch each other will solve this problem immediately.

It is not only the horizontal profile of the chewing surface in the incisors that plays an important role in the state of the teeth. The vertical surface plays an equally important part. The lower jaw, when seen from the side, changes its state more rapidly in the horizontal direction than the upper jaw. The front edges of the lower incisors become blunt. A rearwards adjustment of the lower jaw is encouraged. The forward gliding movement of the lower jaw against the upper jaw can no longer take place. When the horse is asked to work "on the bit," the lower jaw is pushed to the back, and the tension caused in the jaw joint increases to the point of agony. The chewing surface

an inclination of the chewing surface. Many horses have a favorite direction of chewing and wear the teeth correspondingly more on one side than on the other. The gradient of the slope will become more pronounced with time.

The same rule applies here: the earlier the balance is restored in the chewing surface, the smaller the repercussions on the chewing activities and the irregular wear of the single teeth.

A special float is used for the incisors and the longer teeth are shortened on the left, right and on top as well as below.

Wrong feeding can also be instrumental in wearing down the incisors

The incisors of the upper jaw are often not worn consistently. The lower jaw will get pushed back further and further through the overbite of the upper incisors.

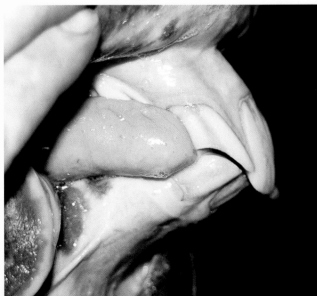

of the upper incisors gets so distorted that the fronts do not get worn anymore and therefore grow impossibly long. The lower jaw is displaced further and further to the back.

Shortening and balancing the upper incisors and stabilizing the chewing surface of the lower incisors can allow for the relocation of the lower jaw to the front.

Some horses, especially those which are stabled all day, display vices like crib-biting, windsucking and scraping the door with the upper incisors.

When a horse crib-bites or wind-sucks, it will bite the manger or other objects in the stable, lean on the object and swallow air with an obvious grunting noise. This vice can go on for hours on end and in extreme cases without interruption. The teeth are sometimes worn down to the extent of exposing the pulp. These horses have a noticeably reduced feed intake because of the discomfort caused by their teeth. Once the pulp of the tooth is exposed, complication in the form of infection is certain.

The treatment is to prevent the horses from cribbing. Remove from the stable all possible objects on which the horse can bite. Painting "anti-crib paste" on the door and bars of the stable often has no noticeable effect. Special cribbing collars can be successful. The best therapy for these horses is intensive preoccupation through movement, turning out in paddocks and an abundance of activity and entertainment in and around the stable. Changing the horse into an open box can be of further assistance. There is also an operation that can be done to prevent the horse from swallowing air. This operation is successful in 75 percent of cases.

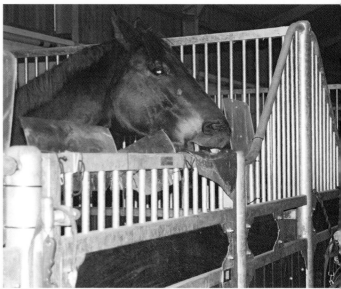

Through biting on objects the crib-biter will wear down the incisors of the upper jaw. In extreme cases the pulp of the teeth will be exposed. This will lead to infection.

Scraping the teeth means just that. The horse scrapes the incisors against the lattice structure between the boxes or the steel plate on the stable door. They put their incisors on the object, without opening the mouth, and slide across the object with light pressure. They either move only the head and neck, or as with weaving, transfer their weight from one front leg to the other. Horses with this problem have their upper and lower incisors worn down on the front edges. Depending on the technique the horse uses, the teeth can also be worn down just on the upper incisors. The treatment is much the same as with crib-biting. Removing all objects from the stable, while providing entertainment, movement, and a change in the routine, is the best therapy against this vice and to halt further wear on the teeth.

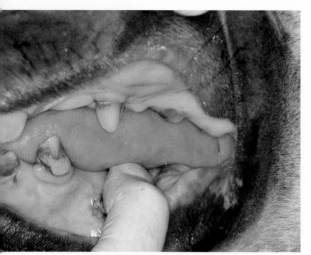

A sharp canine

Canine being burred down

A canine that has been burred down to the niveau of the gum

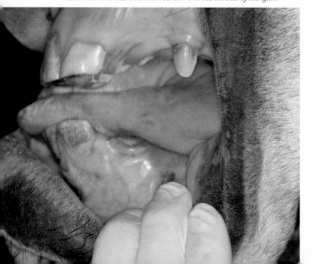

The canine – former fighting tooth

The canine tooth, originally a fighting tooth, can still be quite big and angular in some horses. The canines have no chewing surface, but jut out into a peak in the mouth. The front and back side can, depending on the construction of the tooth, have definite sharp edges. When examining the mouth, one can incur serious injuries on these sharp edges. The tongue fills out the space between the canines and can be badly irritated and even severely injured by the sharp edges on the canines. The bit also presses on the tongue. The tongue tries to escape this pressure by moving to the front and the back of the mouth. The top and bottom of the mouth is restricted by the upper and lower jawbones, making it impossible to escape the pressure to these areas. The sideways escape route pushes the tongue into clear contact with the canines. When these teeth have sharp edges, it can lead to a painful reaction in the ridden horse.

Concealed canines are teeth that have not yet developed and have not erupted through the gum. Canines have a very big, long root, and this can give rise to uncomfortable reactions when there are disruptions in the phase of development. Horses with concealed canines are poor eaters and show serious defense reactions when bridled. When manually examining the horse, modest pressure on the interdental space of the lower jaw will cause severe discomfort. The build-up of tartar can cause inflammation in the area where the visible crown makes the transition to the gum (see page 62 on tartar).

Canines can be burred into a rounder shape or even right down to the niveau of the gums.

Canines do not continue to erupt, which means a single treatment, for example burring it down, will solve the problem for the rest of the horse's life.

> The canine was originally a fighting tooth. Today it is still a very distinct tooth and can be extremely sharp. This tooth can be shortened up to the niveau of the gums.

The wolf tooth – an unpopular leftover

The first premolar is known as the wolf tooth, and is a leftover tooth in horses. This tooth is found directly in front of the first "real" premolar in the upper jaw and only occasionally in the lower jaw. Not every horse develops a wolf tooth. This small leftover will only seldom reach the gum and protrudes as a small, pointed tooth in the interdental space. If the wolf tooth is directly in front of the first premolar, it will, for the most part, not trouble the horse when it consumes its food. As soon as the bridle is put on, however, the tongue is displaced forward and down. In the same way as already described with the canines, the upper and lower jaws restrict the mouth. The tongue has to move away sideways from the pressure exerted and then comes into contact with the wolf tooth. This tooth is very sharp and can cut the tongue. The horse will refuse to go along with being bridled up. The ridden horse is understandably resistant in these circumstances and puts up an even greater fight when the reins are taken up; the pressure on the tongue is intensified and this is all pressed against the sharp wolf tooth.

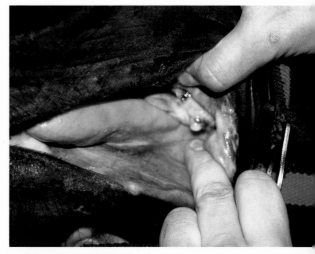
A wolf tooth in the upper jaw

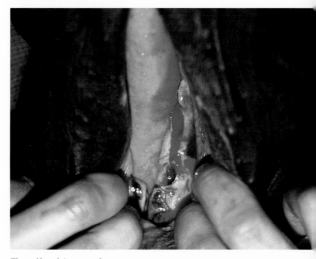
The wolf tooth is removed.

A wolf tooth with a short root

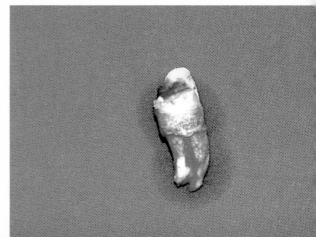

Wolf teeth only have a remnant of a root. The removal of a wolf tooth is easily accomplished as a routine in a sedated, standing horse. It is recommended to remove this tooth as a preventative measure.

Sometimes one will find a wolf tooth that has grown into the bone of the upper jaw. When removing such a tooth, it could break off at this junction. The gum will heal rapidly over this area. Within eight days the horse will be all but perfectly inured to this. If the tooth breaks off above the niveau of the gum, a sharp end can result, and this must be removed.

Concealed wolf teeth are insufficiently developed teeth. They stay put under the gums and can cause a great deal of pain through the pressure from the bit in the ridden horse. With adequate pressure from the fingers, one can feel the bump under the gum, and the horses will mainly react with sensitivity. X-rays can remove any doubt about the existence of a concealed wolf tooth. Removal of the concealed wolf tooth can sometimes miraculously solve problems in the ridden horse.

The wolf tooth, as first premolar, is a leftover tooth and possesses a short root. This tooth often interferes with riding. Removal of the tooth is uncomplicated, and the wound heals within a few days.

Dental cement defects

Dental cement is a reasonably soft substance in the tooth in relation to the other substances. It is the material that fills the gap between the enamel and the coating of the root. If this cement is not properly formed, it can break down on the chewing surfaces of the teeth. Food particles will get caught in these spaces where cement has been lost, leading to tooth decay. In advanced cases, this infection can penetrate the pulp of the tooth. This results in an infection that can only be treated under costly circumstances. The end result is usually the loss of the tooth through infection of the pulp and root or breakage of the tooth.

Recognizing this condition early is the only way in which relevant preventive treatment can be given. These changes can be diagnosed in the yearly examination of the teeth. If defects are discovered on the chewing surfaces of the teeth, they could be filled using special procedures. Only the most extreme cases are treated, however. Normally the continuous eruption of the tooth will supply fresh tooth to replace the defect.

Caries (tooth decay)

Caries, also known as tooth decay, can develop from the cement defects described above. As a rule the infection will damage the tooth substance in the area of the visible crown. This is then visible as black

Caries does not occur in horses as it does in humans. The continuous eruption of the tooth means that new tooth substance is always available. However, serious caries in horses will often lead to the spontaneous breakage of the tooth.

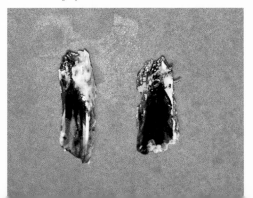

discoloration around the border of the crown or on the chewing surface of the tooth. The tooth, more specifically the tooth cement, is damaged through the process of decay. This kind of disease is very rare in horses, but when it does occur it is more often found in M1. Horses have the advantage over humans that their teeth continually erupt, and so new tooth substance is always available. This means that a disease like caries has relatively little effect, for it does not really have a chance to get establish-ed. Treatment is similar to that for the cement defects.

Pulpitis (root canal inflammation)

Pulpitis is the inflammation of the pulp of the tooth. The pulp is the supply canal for the tooth, with blood vessels, lymph vessels and nerve cells run-ning through it. It is the "living" part of the tooth. The pulp ranges from the tip of the root up through to the reserve crown of the tooth. The continual eruption of the tooth means the pulp is always being pushed up into the direction of the chewing surface. In order to prevent the opening of the pulp, secondary dentine will close this aperture. If the pulp opening is exposed, either through breakage of the tooth, degeneration of the chewing surface or damage to the socket of the tooth, the bacteria present in the mouth will in all likelihood cause an infection of the pulp. This infection will inevitably lead to painful inflammation, and a swelling will appear on the gum in the area of the root. This swelling cannot expand to the outside and will put pressure on the nerve in the pulp. Intense pain is the result. Advanced inflammation will result in the tooth dying.

Inflammation of the pulp can have various causes. Fractures of a tooth through a kick or biting on hard objects are among the most common causes of pul-pitis. In some cases it can also be caused by extreme caries or a cement defect that is so deep as to affect the pulp. Irregular wear through faulty positioning of the teeth or heavy grinding are mechanical ways of opening the pulp. The tooth is worn down quick-er than normal, and the closing of the pulp with the secondary dentine is not rapid enough. Germs can then find their way into the pulp. The wear on the back surfaces of displaced teeth can, in extreme cases, also lead to the opening of the pulp (and infection). To prevent this from happening, the pro-truding and displaced tooth should be shortened accordingly. Acute infections of the teeth do not necessarily mean the horse will become gravely ill. A healthy immune system and good oral hygiene will lead to a speedy and often spontaneous reco-very of the pulp after mechanical opening.

Infection of the pulp can also very occasionally be the result of a general infection in the vascular system.

Periodontitis

Periodontitis is the inflammation of the soft tissue around the tooth. In most cases bacteria that pene-trate the area of the socket surrounding the tooth cause this infection. This infection will intensify and will break down the structures that hold the tooth in place, as well as the supporting bone around the tooth. A build-up of pus occurs that can burst towards the outside of the mouth. This is the development of a so-called fistula. In the upper jaw these fistulas can connect to the maxillary sinuses and lead to festering in the sinuses. This is evident in an unpleasant, foul-smelling discharge from one nostril.

Inflammation of the soft tissue around the tooth can be the result of penetration of food substances like grains, hard wood pieces or other objects into the gums. Feeding of molasses or other sweet sugary food promotes, as in humans, the beginning of periodontitis.

Bacteria have a bias towards sugar, which assists in the growth process. Horses with cavities in their teeth are especially at risk from periodontitis.

In some cases, for example after a blow to the head, inflammation of the soft tissue around the tooth can occur spontaneously without the participation of germs. This can then lead to infection of the injured soft tissue when the injury is not treated appropriately.

Advanced inflammation of the soft tissue around the tooth is incredibly tenacious and can only be treated using intensive therapy. Cleaning the inflamed area thoroughly and antibiotic therapy do not always solve the problem. Extraction of the tooth is often the only solution. Waiting too long to administer the treatment can result in the neighboring teeth being affected. It is clear that professional assistance must be sought sooner rather than later.

The shedding of teeth, the removal of primary teeth, and the presence of irregular teeth will all tend to encourage the possibility of infection in the soft tissue and ultimately in the tooth itself.

Removal of a primary tooth will leave a gap in the gum, in which food particles can be caught. The deeper the pit, the tighter food particles can be impacted into it, and the less likely it is to clear by itself. The result is inevitably an infection of the socket and the bone of the jaw. If the infection is severe, it can lead to the complete loss of the erupting permanent tooth. Oral hygiene is as important in the horse as in humans. The primary teeth will be shed between two and four and a half years of age, and during this time the incisors should be inspected on a regular basis, and food particles should be removed from the pockets in the gums.

The molars can also get food stuck between and around them, causing inflammation in these areas. Controlling these areas is more difficult. In the course of routine examinations, the way the molars are aligned should be given special attention. When a tooth is not exactly within the dental arcade (row of teeth), but is slightly out of alignment, causing crowding of the teeth, the possibility of food getting stuck is higher, and therefore the risk of infection is greater.

Awareness of the danger, cleaning and treatment are the best prevention against infection. These should be done in connection with routine veterinary care.

Problems when shedding teeth

In the young animal the incisors and the premolars are present as primary or milk teeth. When the horse develops into a mature animal, the milk teeth will be shed, and the permanent teeth will take their

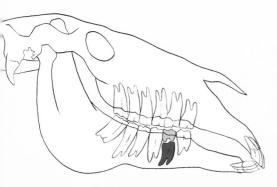

Fixed, wedged milk tooth cap on the P3. This is called a riding cap.

place. This transition to the second dentition can, as is the case with children, be accompanied by many painful problems. The caps of the milk teeth can be too tight and cause great pressure on the erupting second tooth. These caps that stay put on the newly erupted teeth are called retained caps.

Pushing the milk tooth out of its space can put incredible pressure on the new secondary tooth. The inflamation of the surrounding tissue can be very painful. Horses in this situation will eat poorly. They are normally between two and four years old. This is also the age at which horses start their education under a rider. Fighting the bit is a common problem, often connected with shedding of the teeth.

Milk teeth caps of the upper and lower premolars. The cap of the upper tooth is wider than that of the lower tooth.

Removal of the milk teeth caps is the easiest solution for this problem. This should, however, only be done once the cap is already pushed out into the mouth, or if it is mobile. The milk tooth has an important protecting function as regards the developing permanent tooth underneath it. If this function is interrupted by the premature removal of the milk tooth, there can be insufficient growth and eventual infection of the permanent tooth. The inadequately developed cementum in the permanent tooth can not substitute as a satisfactory barrier against the germs in the mouth. Bacteria in the mouth can infect the tooth and penetrate the pulp. Infection of the pulp is always a complicated problem.

Loose caps on the premolars frequently will not fall off but can slide sideways off the permanent crown and be caught between the neighboring teeth. The edges of the caps are razor-sharp. If the cap is caught at an angle between the neighboring teeth, it will injure the tongue on the one side and the cheek on the other. When the outside of the cheek is touched, the horse will react violently. Removal of the caps is a fast and effective treatment and will give immediate relief.

Permanent incisors will also replace primary incisors. They too will get pushed out into the mouth by the erupting permanent tooth. In some cases the erupting permanent tooth does not sit exactly

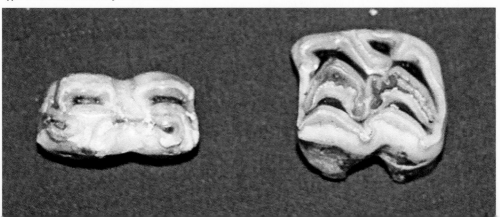

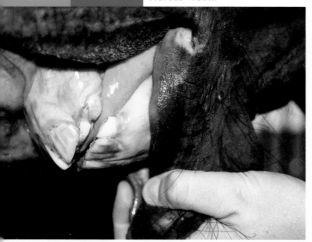

The permanent teeth do not always push out the primary incisors. The primary and permanent teeth often stand in two rows next to each other, with the milk teeth in the front row. In this photograph the permanent corner incisor developed behind the milk tooth. The milk tooth is compressed between the two permanent teeth.

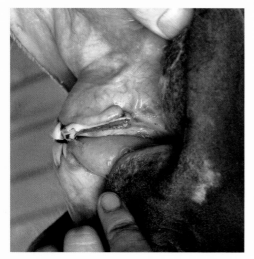

A slanted primary corner incisor. It will not be pushed out by the permanent tooth.

beneath the milk tooth, and will then push through behind the milk tooth. A double row of teeth will result, with the primary teeth in the front row and the permanent teeth in the back row. The horse will not necessarily suffer tenderness in this case. It is recommended, however, to remove the primary teeth in order for the permanent teeth to move into the correct positions.

Occasionally the roots of the milk teeth will not atrophy. They remain next to the permanent incisors and thwart the formation of a uniform chewing surface.

These primary teeth should be removed to allow the permanent teeth to move into their correct positions. Removal of these milk teeth will be more difficult, for they still have their roots intact. Breaking a root during extraction is a complication. Removing a fractured root is a troublesome activity for the veterinarian.

The canines are present as milk teeth, but they never erupt into the mouth. They always remain buried under the gum. The permanent canines also often have trouble breaking through the gum. They can stay under the gums as well, and cause severe pressure, which results in soreness. Light massaging of the gums can encourage the teeth to break through the gum. If this does not help within two days, a small incision can be made in the gum to facilitate the eruption of the tooth.

Tartar

Tartar is found in the horse, but in contrast to the tartar of meat eaters, it has a less significant clini-

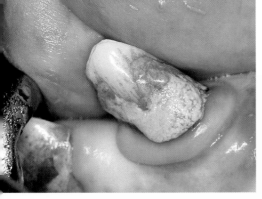

The canine teeth in particular, have a ring of limescale around them, also called tartar. This irritates the gum at the base of the tooth. Removing the tartar is relatively easy using a chisel or other hard instrument.

cal importance. Tartar often develops on the teeth that are in the area where the salivary ducts open into the mouth. Tartar is mainly found on the canines and on the incisors. In older horses with irregular teeth like a wave or step mouth, tartar can also develop on the outside of the molars.

Tartar is a yellow-brown coating around the tooth where the visible crown meets with the gum. Deposits from food can give the tartar a green to black color. Tartar consists of limescale and has the consistency of pumice. Chalky food will promote the formation of tartar. In extreme cases the tartar will extend from the gum to about the middle of the visible tooth. Tartar does not develop on the chewing surface of the tooth.

The porous quality of tartar means it can be removed easily from a tooth, using a small chisel. The best way of removing it, however, is with an

ultrasonic scaling apparatus. The ultrasonic noise is often disturbing for the horse, and the scaling process has to take place under sedation. To prevent new tartar build-up, the surface of the tooth can be smoothed.

Gaps between the teeth

Food can get stuck in gaps between the teeth and can cause infection of the gum or socket of the tooth. In most cases gaps will appear due to the absence of teeth. Broken off teeth, teeth that are too small, and teeth that have moved will also cause gaps. Delayed development of the permanent tooth can cause a sensitive, exposed gap when the primary tooth falls out. Regular cleaning of gaps can prevent infection.

What are bumps?

Bumps are the bony swellings found usually on the lower jaw. They are sometimes also found in the upper jaw in the vicinity of the front molars. It is often thought that these bumps are the result of a kick or blow; they are, however, formed during the developing phase of the tooth. The bumps are visible from the second to sixth year. This is the time when the permanent tooth is developing. The unshed milk teeth and narrow socket hamper the eruption of the permanent tooth. The developing permanent tooth and the periodontal structures (all the tissues surrounding the tooth) including the bone of the jaw are subjected to increased pressure. The reaction is localized swelling in the area of the roots.

A gap between the intermediate and corner incisors

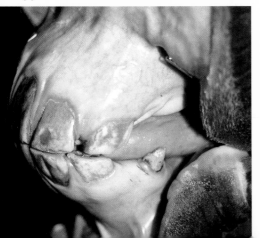

Young horses produce permanent teeth and these teeth erupt into the mouth. When the socket is too narrow or the milk tooth is still too tight in its space, the resulting pressure will cause a reaction in the jawbone. These reactions are visible as so-called bumps on the lower jaw.

The bumps are sometimes known as false cysts, and they disappear after a certain amount of time. They are occasionally sensitive to touch but are not usually a medical problem. In isolated cases it can happen that the thin layer of bone underneath the root of the tooth causes inflammation. The bumps can then be extremely painful and develop a lesion from which a slimy secretion is produced. This situation naturally calls for veterinary care.

Swellings in the upper jaw are not often visible on the outside. The bumps can expand to the inside of the jaw where they will fill the space of the maxillary sinuses. These horses make an obvious noise when breathing. Once the bumps disappear, the noise will mostly vanish as well.

Treatment of bumps is not necessary as a rule, for the bony reactions will cease once the tooth reaches its final position in the jaw.

Bipolar magnetic fields will accelerate the regeneration of the bone.

Surplus teeth

The adult horse has up to 40 teeth, including the four canines that are not present in every horse. In many cases the wolf tooth develops in front of the first "real" molar. This problem has already been discussed. Occasionally there will be a fourth molar (M4). This extra molar does not have an opposing tooth, which means it does not get worn like the rest. This tooth will continue erupting and eventually will press on the gum of the opposite jaw. This makes chewing painful. The mechanical damage causes food particles to get caught in the broken skin. The result is a foul-smelling inflammation and a great deal of discomfort. Horses with this problem are poor eaters, have shaggy coats and resist the aids of the rider.

Noticing this extra tooth is not as easy as it sounds. The chewing surfaces of the row of molars have an upward curve towards the back of the mouth. It is only possible to see in this area when the horse's mouth is opened extremely wide, and with the help of a good headlamp. The easiest and most effective way to achieve this is by using the mouth speculum. (See p. 111ff.) The jaw can then be opened wide enough. The row of teeth can be palpated right up to the very last tooth. The surplus tooth (M4) must be manually shortened or surgically removed.

A horse has six incisors in both the upper and the lower jaw. Occasionally an extra incisor may be present. This extra tooth has no clinical significance and is often spotted only by accident, if at all.

A surplus tooth structure can also be found in an entirely different position on the horse's head. Ear fistulas are examples of surplus tooth structures. Due to faulty positioning, this tooth is sometimes found in an embryonic state under the ear of the horse. These horses will have a small, oozing wound at the base of the ear that will not heal. Beneath the fistula there is a solid object, the tooth structure. The final diagnosis can only be made by X-ray. Surgical removal is the answer.

Many tooth structures are also shifted in their position in the mouth. It is possible for the canine to develop next to the corner incisor or the first premolar. The canine has a longer root and is not extracted as easily as the wolf tooth. The canine is noticeably bigger than, and therefore easily distinguished from, the wolf tooth.

Missing teeth

Mares often do not have canine teeth. This tooth, originally a fighting tooth, has no specific role anymore. The modern horse does not have to defend itself against predators. Valuable teeth, however, also can be missing. Foals and yearlings often get injuries through kicks when they play in the paddocks. The tooth structure can get so badly damaged by these injuries that a permanent incisor might be destroyed completely. This will result in a space in the region of the incisors. Technically it may be possible to overcome such defects, but from a medical point of view this is not essential. A strict oral hygiene regime is recommended in these cases. Watch out that the tooth opposing the gap does not over-erupt and thereby affect the chewing ability.

A consequence of a missing tooth is that the opposing tooth does not wear, and needs to be manually floated at least once a year.

In various diseases of the molars the tooth structures sometimes have to be surgically removed. Regular dental inspection is necessary to prevent eruption of opposing teeth into these spaces.

This tooth structure was surgically removed from the base of the ear of a horse. Surplus teeth appear in this position due to faulty positioning in the embryonic stage.

Incorrect positioning of teeth

On examination of the mouth, teeth that grow at right angles to the others are easily distinguished. In many instances the lower molar (M1) will grow sideways in the direction of the cheek. The chewing surface is not on top, and thus it will not get ground down by the opposing tooth in the upper jaw. This crooked tooth will continue to grow in the direction of the cheek, and the tooth opposite will over-erupt due to insufficient wear.

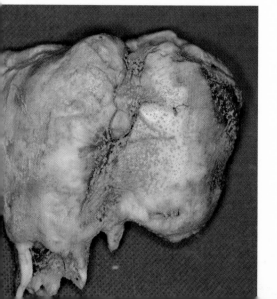

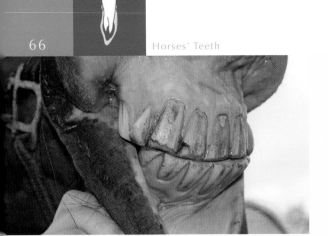

This horse has seven incisors in the upper jaw.

Due to the pressure from the molars in the upper jaw, the crooked tooth in the lower jaw will be pushed further into the cheek, irritating the skin more and more. This can result in the tooth breaking the skin of the cheek, and the bacteria present in the mouth may cause a serious infection of the mucous membranes of the cheeks and the chewing muscles. The tooth from the upper jaw exerts such intense pressure on the crooked tooth that the mere act of chewing will cause extreme discomfort. Understandably, the horse will not want to eat. Experience has taught that incorrect positioning of teeth is more or less ignored and not seen as a disease.

Tooth fractures

The material that the tooth consists of, especially the enamel, is extremely hard but also brittle. The enamel of the molars of the upper jaw is particularly brittle, and as a result there are more fractures of teeth in the upper jaw. The incisors and the lower molars are more susceptible to fractures by a blow or kick to the head.

There is a definite distinction between a crack, which does not split the tooth, and a fracture. The overall shape of the tooth is retained if it cracks. If only a piece of the tooth breaks off, it is called a chipped tooth. Complete fractures occur along the length or across the tooth.

Fractures happen mostly through trauma like a kick, or even the use of incorrect mouth speculums. A fracture of the incisors is easily detected. If a piece of the tooth is missing or the whole tooth is at an angle to the rest of the teeth, a fracture is indicated. A fracture is often sharp and cuts the tongue or cheeks. The most difficult fracture to detect is when the break is on the reserve crown or root. An exact diagnosis can then only be made with the help of an X-ray.

A tear in the gum can accompany fractures. This can lead to infection in the area of the socket. Fractures of molars are accompanied by symptoms such as a bad smell from the mouth and uneasy chewing, similar to when hooks and ramps are present.

A horse with an acute fracture will experience discomfort when drinking cold water. If the visible crown breaks off and the pulp is exposed this can result in infection of the root canal inside the tooth. A surgical extraction should be carried out in this situation.

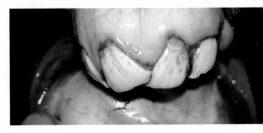

Another horse can kick out the incisors. If a tooth is missing, it means the opposing tooth has nothing to grind against. Regular control and correction of the opposing tooth is crucial.

Diseases of the mouth

Faulty position of the jaw

The jaws can be of differing lengths. Too short a lower jaw is called a parrot mouth. The general term for this faulty jaw development is an underbite. Too long a lower jaw in relation to the upper jaw is called a pig mouth, or overbite. Incorrect location of the jaw may cause intense irritation of the mucous membranes of the opposing jaws. The teeth will not be worn down under these circumstances. A severe inflammation of the mucous membranes is the consequence and may result in irritation of the jawbone itself. This incorrect positioning of the jaw is not restricted to the region of the incisors, but the abnormal relationship may also be present in the area of the first and last molars. These horses have obvious pain, refuse to eat and are impossible to ride. The most important therapy is the floating of the unworn crown on the projecting incisors or molars. Examination of the protruding teeth should take place every six months at the least. Floating the erupting crowns will prevent damage to the mucous membranes.

Twisted growth of the upper jaw is seldom seen in horses. In these horses regular floating of the incisors and molars must be performed. Grinding down of the teeth will only take place in some of the teeth. In order to prevent the extreme eruption of teeth, they have to be floated on a regular basis.

Pig mouth – the lower jaw is longer than the upper jaw.

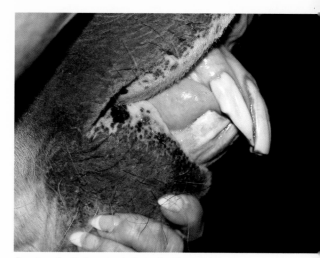

Parrot mouth – the lower jaw is shorter than the upper jaw.

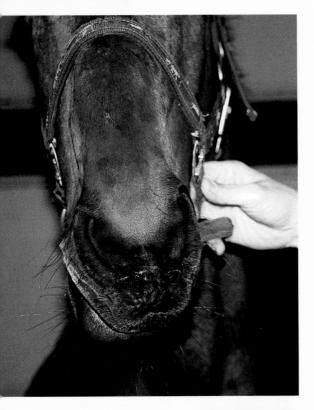

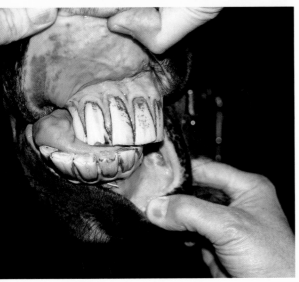

This horse has a twisted upper jaw. The incisors are not edge-to-edge. The molars will be worn only on the one side. Regular floating of the teeth will correct irregular wear.

Fractures of the jaw

A distinction is made between open fractures, covered fractures and a crack of the jaw.

In an open fracture, the bone is not covered and therefore protected by the mucous membrane of the mouth. This is the most complicated fracture of the jaw.

The covered fracture is protected by a still intact mucous membrane. The mucous membrane will prevent bacteria of the mouth from penetrating the crevice of the fracture. The danger of infection is greatly reduced.

A crack in the jaw is described as a division in the jaw that has not shattered through the whole of the jaw. The broken pieces lie in a normal position to each other and are not movable.

Jaw fractures are often found in the lower jaw. They can be the result of a kick to the jaw, or perhaps getting it caught in the partitioning rails of the stable. The lower jaw will break effortlessly at its narrowest part, between the incisors and the molars. In some cases only the dental arcade of the incisors will fracture, or single teeth will be broken out from the jaw. A broken jaw is extremely painful, and depending on where the fracture is, the jaw or the dental arcade will simply hang down.

The fractured part of the bone can be moved to and fro. As is the case with tongue injuries and general injuries of the mouth, the healing of jaw fractures is exceptionally fast. Intensive blood flow to the area and the disinfecting effect of the saliva will support the rapid healing of fractures.

Depending on the way the jaw fractured, it is often possible to mend the jaw without surgical

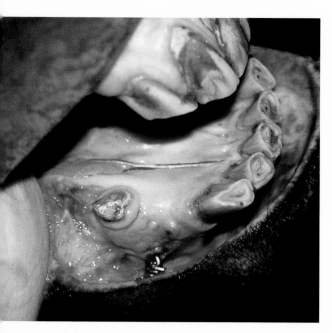

...er jaw is relatively thin and can break easily. Clever work ...e can help stabilize and heal the jaw.

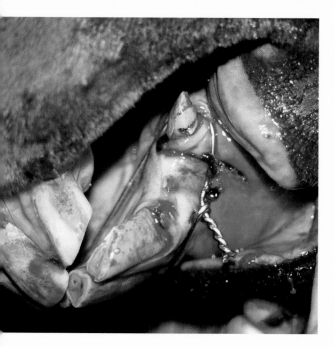

intervention. This way of resolving the problem is only feasible in cracks, splits in the bone and covered fractures. If the bone is fractured right through and the wound is open, the break should be stabilized. This normally is by means of surgical procedures, using wire, plates, screws or outside fixation. These techniques will not be discussed in detail; they involve specialist treatment by a veterinarian with specialized skills.

Fractures of the branches of the lower jaw and the upper jaw are more dramatic. These kinds of fractures occur through blows, severe falls and car accidents. The horse will be unable to eat; the broken part of the jaw will be enormously painful when touched, and when the jaws are moved against each other, a crunching sound can be heard. Immediate veterinary care is essential.

Diseases of the jaw joint

As described earlier, the jaw joint is relatively high up and approximately 5 cm behind the outside corner of the eye. In this position the joint is comparatively exposed. It is covered merely by skin and protrudes a little on the outside of the bony part of the horse's head. If the horse is cast and cannot get up, it might bash its head against the stable wall or floor and injure the jaw joint in this way. The jaw joint, like any other joint, is filled with a liquid. When the joint capsule is broken, this amber-colored liquid will flow out of the wound. Dirt and bacteria can now get into the capsule, causing infection of the joint. It is of the utmost importance that treatment is given as soon as possible. Dealing with it within 24 hours is normally quite effective. The joint must be rinsed; all possible broken bony pieces must be removed, and antibiotic cover must be given. The longer treatment is delayed, the greater the chance of a serious infection that will impart ongoing problems.

The jaw joint can also be damaged with obtuse violence like a kick or blow to the head. This may not open the joint. If the joint capsule is squashed, the skin might be broken and the supporting structures stretched. The joint causes discomfort, and the horse chews in a restrained manner. This is difficult to diagnose. Touching the joint will point to the tender areas. Pushing on the joint will provoke fierce defensive reactions. In such circumstances the possibility of a joint fracture must be investigated. An X-ray will shed light on the matter. In the event of a positive diagnosis of a fracture, rubbing in some topical anti-inflammatory cream can help to calm the ache in the jaw relatively quickly.

Horses with pain in the jaw joint must be fed with soft food like mash. These horses should not be ridden, as taking up the reins will put pressure on the jaw joint and this pain will make the horse difficult to work with.

The jaw joint is not a true hinge joint. It moves up and down and also to a lesser degree sideways. This mobility increases the danger of dislocation. If the horse bites on a large, hard object on one side, this uneven burden on the jaw can cause just the one side to dislocate. A kick on the jaw from another horse can actually dislocate both sides of the jaw. The lower jaw will hang limp with both the single and double dislocations, and the mouth will be half open. When the jaw is moved manually during an examination, the horse will exhibit signs of severe pain. The jaw can only be relocated under general anaesthetic. This is a risky and difficult treatment. The prognosis can only be thought of as good once the relocation is successful and no fracture of the joint is visible.

The various problems outlined above and uneven dentition can impose damaging loads on the jaw joint. In the long term this can lead to jaw joint arthrosis (chronic joint inflammation).

Horses with this problem are poor eaters. They bite their food, but do not grind it. Moving the jaw on a horizontal plane will be agonizing for them. Jaw joint arthrosis is seldom diagnosed. The best prevention is regular correction of faulty dentition. Habitual examination and correction will avert degenerative, abrasive changes such as arthrosis of the jaw joint. Once arthrosis has been diagnosed, the discomfort can be treated with medication to relieve most of the pain.

Inflammation of the sinuses

The sinuses of the horse are made up of the two maxillary sinuses on the side of the skull plus the frontal sinus in the middle of the skull. They are large cavities filled with air. The roots of the teeth of the young horse project into these cavities. An infection in the mouth or in the nose can cause inflammation of the maxillary sinuses. Advanced infection of the maxillary sinuses can also involve the frontal sinus.

A noticeable symptom of a sinus infection is above all a foul-smelling discharge from the nose. These horses will make a snorting noise when breathing. If you knock on the side that is inflamed, you will hear a dull muffled sound in the area of the sinus. Horses with an infection in the sinuses will react with apparent defensiveness. Closer inspection of the molars may reveal foreign bodies in the sockets, broken teeth and gum infection as the reason for an advanced infection in the maxillary sinuses. When there is no specific indication of an infection from the mouth, there is always the use of X-ray as a further diagnosis to note bony changes and fluid in the sinuses. Once the cause of the infection has been localized, the tooth can be treated or extracted, and the sinuses can be flushed out.

The treatment of sinus infections can be lengthy, and there is always the danger of reinfection. Recognizing the problem early, and speedy treatment, will improve the outcome and minimize the danger of a new infection.

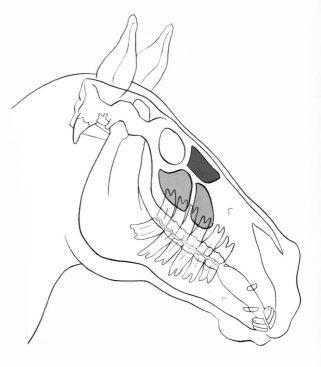

The maxillary sinuses are connected to the nose via a ventilation passage. The roots of P4 to M3 protrude into the maxillary sinuses. There is also a connection to the frontal sinus.

Obstruction and inflammation of the nasolacrimal duct

The nasolacrimal duct runs from the outer corner of the eye in the upper half of the sinuses down into the nostrils. The actual exit of the duct on the surface is visible approximately three to four centimeters from the nostril opening. The nasolacrimal duct redirects the liquid of the tears and drains it in the nostrils.

If this system functions properly, the point where the duct opens in the nostrils will be damp. This duct is often obstructed or narrowed by pressurized conditions in the sinuses. A rise in the pressure on the inside of the sinuses takes place when there is inflammation or infection of the sinuses or the roots of the molars. This will result in an accumulation of pus. The sticky pus will obstruct the entrance from the sinus to the nose. The pressure can become so extreme that the bony cover of the sinus can actually bulge to the outside, forming a visible swelling. In these circumstances the liquid from the tear duct cannot flow through the nasolacrimal duct, and the eye on the affected side will have a permanent flow of liquid. This is called a teary eye.

The nasolacrimal duct itself, however, can also be inflamed and infected. Bacteria from either the eye or the nostrils can cause an infection, followed by coagulation of the tear duct.

Dealing with the cause of the infection by treating the diseased sinus, tooth or nasolacrimal duct will be the prerequisite for healing. It is also important to flush the nasolacrimal duct. Using a large syringe, the liquid is pushed through the opening of the nasolacrimal duct in the nostrils until the liquid exits from the eye.

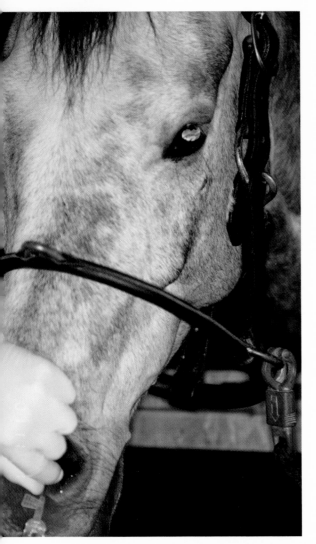

Flushing of the nasolacrimal duct clears away obstructions and allows the flow of tears.

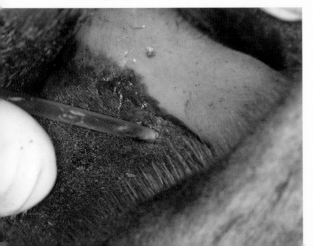

This treatment must be repeated until the naso-lacrimal duct stays open and the liquid from the tear duct flows easily.

Infection of the gum surrounding the tooth

The mouth of the horse is covered by a pale pink mucous membrane that is incredibly sensitive. The mucous membrane surrounding the tooth is called the gingiva (gum). The ingestion of irritating matter, poisons, sharp objects and infectious bacteria can cause inflammation of the mucous membrane.

> *Inflammation of the gingiva has the following symptoms:*
>
> * *redness of the gum with partly open, bloody areas*
> * *swelling of the gum*
> * *loss of gum around the tooth, food particles in these pockets.*

External trauma such as injury through kicks or blows, use of inappropriate bits, roughness from the rider and treatment of the teeth themselves can damage the mucous membrane.

As a rule of thumb, it is said the older a horse, the more sensitive the mucous membrane and the bigger the danger of inflammation and infection.

Inflammation of the gingiva can adversely affect the jawbone and the root of the tooth (periodontitis).

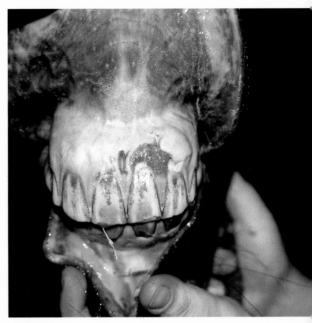

Inflammation of the gingiva of the incisors

Symptoms of inflammation can vary according to the acuteness of the infection. With minor infection it will only be in the form of localized inflammation of the gum. This is called gingivitis, gingiva being the gum and "-itis" the ending for inflammation. Distinct redness and a slight swelling are the symptoms. Sensitivity to touch is negligible. Localized inflammation is mainly caused by the formation of tartar, especially around the canines at the junction of the gum and the tooth. Large accumulations of tartar can bring about a corresponding amount of inflammation.

When a piece of tooth breaks off below the level of the gum, there will be an accumulation of food particles in the open area between tooth and gum. The localized inflammation around this tooth will often penetrate into the deeper levels of the gingiva and reach the bony section of the socket.

There is often a loss of gingiva in circumstances like these. These areas are also tender to the touch. An extremely important criterion is an unpleasant smell from the mouth. The stronger the smell, the higher the degree of infection. Treatment from the veterinarian is necessary in this case. Appropriate cleaning and disinfection with antibacterial preparations aid speedy recovery.

Tooth fractures, where a big piece of the tooth breaks off or the tooth splits in half, will result in bigger cavities where food particles can fall into the depth of the socket and end up at the root of the tooth. The infection will spread fast and will affect the jawbone. Loss of tooth material, root and bone is the result. Horses with an infection in this area have severe discomfort and will eat little or nothing at all. Pressure on the tooth will cause extreme pain. In the examination of these horses the mouth should not be opened. Manual assessment from the out-side will direct the examiner to the painful location. Conservative treatment like bathing the area and use of antibiotic drugs will not be sufficient to heal this. The tooth will most probably, as already discussed in the section on periodontitis, have to be extracted.

Extensive inflammation of the mucous membrane through the intake of poisonous or other irritating substances is visible owing to a reddened, generally painful appearance of the mucous membrane and in extreme cases an increase in production of saliva. In these cases it is recommended to flush the horse's mouth with water and vinegar, treat the gums with a tincture of myrrh and to put the horse on a diet of soft grass and mash. Some horses with an extensive inflammation of the gingiva are so sensitive that they find it impossible to drink water from an automatic drinker. These horses must have a normal bucket of water at their disposal, and one should try and introduce water in the mouth of the horse with a large syringe.

Small blisters on the mucous membrane can develop from a viral infection. This type of infection is particularly difficult to treat but in most cases is not painful. Oral hygiene and the stimulation of the immune system are the best measures. The veterinarian should be consulted in these cases.

Injuries to the bars and corners of the mouth

In many situations the horse will fight against the bit when there is an inflammation or injury present in the corner of the mouth. Injuries often occur in horses that are playful and like to carry objects in their mouths. They chew on the lead, are frightened by something, jump to the side, and the lead tightens. In this scenario, severe injuries to the corner of the mouth, the tongue and mucous membrane on the lower jaw can result. How often does one see horses tied with the bridle? This also can lead to serious injuries. Reins that hang loose and lunge reins clipped onto the bit are both potential dangers for the mouth of the horse. The horse steps on the reins or lunge line; this pulls on the bit; the horse jerks its head up, and an injury to the mouth is the result.

Unfortunately more injuries to the mouth of the horse come from forceful intervention by the rider. Extremely thin bits, exotic nosebands and insensitive riding aids can cause considerable damage to the corners of the mouth.

When such an injury has occurred, the mouth of the horse should be protected, and until healed, no bit should be put in the mouth. In this period of healing the horse can be lunged in a head collar or cavesson and ridden with a bitless bridle. A salve of zinc and cod-liver oil will aid the healing if applied a couple of times a day. The horse may only be ridden on a bit again once the scab has fallen off the wound.

> Forceful riding or tying the horse on the bridle can lead to injuries to the bars of the mouth. The result is often an ugly scar that stays.

Injuries to the lips

The lips of the horse are incredibly sensitive. They consist of various efficient muscles that all work together. Injuries to the lips occur when horses play with each other through the bars that divide the stables. One horse will, for example, bite into the bars, and the neighboring horse will bite the lips of the first one. The veterinarian can stitch the lips with great success. Healing is rapid and without complications when hygiene is good.

Over-tightening of a twitch often injures the top lip. Twitches disturb the flow of blood to the lips. If a twitch is used for longer than 20 minutes on the top lip, the tissue can be damaged in such a way that

it will "die off." At this stage no medical treatment can help. The damaged top lip can just about lose its function. The rule is not to use the twitch for longer than 15-20 minutes at a time and not to roll it too tight. Once it is removed, the top lip must be massaged to stimulate the flow of blood to the area and to minimize injury to the region.

Swelling of the lymph nodes

The palpable lymph nodes that supply the mouth of the horse are in the back half of the lower jaw, between the branches of the jaw. These lymph nodes have the job of transporting away the products of inflammation that are in the region of the teeth and jaws. If an inflammation arises in this area, the lymph nodes will puff up. The lymph nodes below the jaw incorporate many smaller nodes that can swell to the size of a small fist in severe cases of illness. The lymph nodes of young horses can sometimes be swollen due to their higher metabolism. If a horse shows a reaction when the area of the lymph nodes is touched, there is a possibility of localized inflammation. A thorough examination of the mouth and teeth will clarify whether it is a reaction to an illness or in the lymph nodes themselves. A localized reaction of the lymph nodes normally has its origin, via a bacterial infection, in the glands. The lymph nodes will be excruciatingly painful and in advanced cases will be full to bursting.

Once the lymph nodes burst, a sticky, yellow, highly infectious pus will be discharged. This illness occurs mainly in young horses and leaves an almost total immunity against this illness for life.

In this instance the mouth and teeth are not the primary spots where the illnesses come from.

> Swelling of the lymph nodes may be a sign of inflammation in the mouth. In young horses the lymph nodes are often swollen but not painful. This does not mean that there is anything amiss.

Diseases of the tongue

The tongue is a mucous membrane bag stuffed with muscles. The mucous membrane is partly hardened and provides stability to the tongue. The bone of the tongue, the hyoid, imparts mobility, and it is fixed to the skull with soft tissue. The tongue is additionally anchored to the lower jaw with soft tissue. The long tongue muscle runs along the bottom of the neck and reaches the junction with the chest. This muscle aids the movement of the tongue and influences the mechanics of the lower jaw.

Injuries to the tongue can occur with heat, by burning or sharp objects. These injuries can be superficial, only into the mucous membrane, or may go deeper into the muscle of the tongue. Horses that have an extreme inflammation of the tongue overproduce saliva, eat haltingly and are mulish when it comes to putting on the bridle. The danger of the horse's tongue being burned by either hot substances or acid-containing matter is extremely scarce. Horses are incredibly sensitive when it comes to ingesting food. Stinging substances will hardly ever arrive in the horse's mouth, due to the fine selection of food. Mechanical injuries to the horse's tongue are much more common. Foreign bodies such as hard stems and thorns that impale the tongue will inflame it, and the horse will be hypersensitive to this.

Scar on the tongue after healing of an injury.

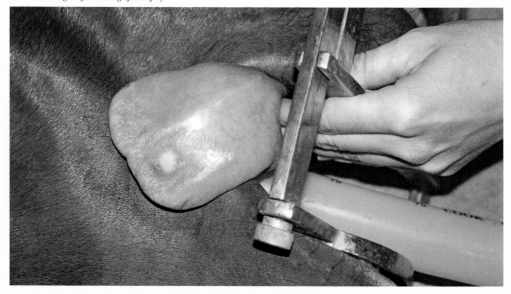

Examination of the mouth and tongue will quickly reveal the cause of the sensitivity, and therefore treatment can be planned accordingly.

Strong bits irritate the mucous membranes not only of the bars of the mouth, but also those of the tongue. One should always take great care that bits do not have rust or sharp edges. Injuries to the tongue can be caused through the careless influence from the rider's hand, but fortunately are rarely seen with today's more sensitive riders.

The conditions are such that the tongue is likely to heal quickly. The circulation of blood is excellent, and there is the added bonus that the saliva has a mild disinfectant quality. In a few cases the tip of the tongue is severed, but that is mostly when the rider has had a fall and the reins get caught around the tongue and the horse then steps on them. The danger of squashing the tongue is greater when curb bits with long leverage and tight curb chains are utilized.

The horse can also bite off the tip of its tongue in a bad fall. The piece that is bitten off is normally so small that it does not make any difference to the function or feeding habits.

Horses use their tongues to feed and drink. The horse can mechanically manage with the loss of about 30 percent of the tongue. It takes up to ten days for the horse to get used to the new length of the tongue, but they have surprisingly little difficulty in coping with the change.

The nerve that supplies the tongue is the hypoglossus (*hypo*=under, *glossus*=tongue). This nerve can be damaged by strangulation, pinning down the head, a blow on the lower jaw or a fracture of the branch of the lower jaw. The nerve can also be damaged by violently pulling the tongue out as a means of discipline, leading to one or both sides being paralysed. The nerve might regenerate within a day, depending on the degree of damage. The horse will not be able to control the tongue while it is healing. It will hang out, either to the front or the side of the mouth. This increases the risk of the horse biting on its tongue. It is also recommended to feed the horse soft food and help it to drink water, suggesting intensive attention. The tongue is not swollen when the nerve has been damaged, and there is no pain.

An abscess or edema of the tongue is quite the opposite of paralysis. The tongue is swollen and very painful under these circumstances. When foreign bodies impale the tongue they can induce infection, abscesses and boils. The tongue swells; the mouth cavity is not big enough to accommodate the oversized volume and the tongue bulges out of the mouth. A similar situation is visible with a squashed tongue. The compressed part, mostly the tip of the tongue, will swell and protrude out of mouth. The situation is improved rapidly when the abscess is lanced and the tongue rinsed with cold water.

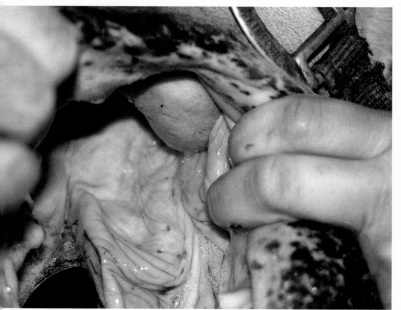

The tip of the tongue can be lost due to injury.
A horse can compensate for 30 percent loss of the tongue.

Rinsing the tongue with cold water from a hose can mean that the horse will drink too much water. In order to prevent this, use a large syringe to spray water in the mouth from the sides.

Functional disorders of the tongue due to central nervous system illnesses like tumors, poisoning and serious infectious illnesses are fortunately very rarely seen.

Fracture of the hyoid

The bone of the tongue is well protected between the branches of the lower jaw. In extremely rare cases, for example a fracture of the lower jaw, the hyoid bone can also be fractured, but this is un- likely to happen. If the tongue is violently pulled out of the mouth as a means of disciplining, this brute force

can actually fracture the hyoid. Treatment is difficult and can only be done under general anaesthetic. Broken pieces and cartilage residue are removed and the fractured bone is stabilized with wire. This kind of operation is only successful when performed immediately after the injury. The longer the wait, the higher the risk of infection.

Tumors in the mouth

In isolated cases tumors can develop in the tooth structure. These involve the enamel, dentine and cement of the tooth, are mostly nonmalignant and can be surgically removed.

Tumours of the soft tissue of the tongue, gingiva and palate, on the other hand, are often aggressive and can be transferred to the lymph nodes, forming secondary growths. The prognosis is poor.

The bone of the jaw can also show tumorous degeneration. The jawbone will actually inflate under these circumstances. Such bony enlargements are not painful at first. It is only when the swelling is massive that the pressure on the neighboring tissue becomes more intense. The horse will then react violently to touch. These varieties of tumors are somewhat infrequent.

Injury and infection of the chewing muscles

The big chewing muscles are on the outside of the head, rendering them more vulnerable to injury. If a horse is cast and knocks its head on the floor, or has wedged its head between two items, these muscles can easily be squashed. Another possibility is when the mouth speculum is opened too wide. This will overstretch the muscle and trigger small tears in the fibers. These horses will feed haltingly and not grind their food properly. Healing can take several days or even weeks. Cooling the muscles can improve the situation. Damage in this way will eventually heal suitably. Massive scar tissue and calcification of the muscle can result in permanent damage. Chewing for these horses is so painful that they will have to be fed a soft diet for the rest of their lives.

Any piercing of the chewing muscle by foreign bodies can, as is the case with the tongue, form an abscess in the muscle. Contagious bacteria can be passed on via foreign bodies or through injuries that rupture the outside skin. The result is almost always localized infection, together with a boil or abscess. Within a few days this abscess will mature and form a barrier around the infection. The barrier will distend (hopefully) towards the outside, where it will burst or be lanced by a veterinarian. The pus will drain and the wound will heal, if kept clean by rinsing it thoroughly with water or a mild disinfectant. It will sometimes happen that the affected muscle does not develop an abscess. The soft tissue is simply inflamed. Antibiotics are the best way to treat this infection and aid in the healing process.

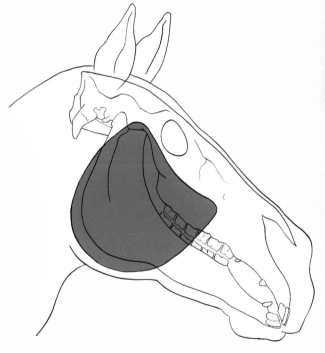

The chewing muscle of the horse

In the case of both the abscess and the inflamed soft tissue, the chewing muscle will swell up. When viewed from the front, the face of the horse is asymmetrical. The swollen side will be painful.

The most important measure to be taken in the case of infection is the removal of the foreign body or whatever has caused the infection. Sharp teeth are often the cause of injury to the mucous membranes of the cheek. Floating the teeth can resolve the problem. When these origins of the problem cannot be eliminated, the consequence is renewed irritation and infection of the mucous membrane and the chewing muscles.

Tetanus can cause spasms in the chewing muscles. The muscles become rigid and instead of bulging out due to infection, the muscles actually fall in. The horse cannot eat or drink under theses circumstances.

Spasms of the muscles can also be caused by botulism food poisoning. This can happen when horses ingest silage containing the remains of dead animals (like rats).

The best prevention is to regularly vaccinate horses against tetanus. Having tests done on the silage is another way to help in the prevention of botulism. Treatment in both cases is difficult, and unfortunately these diseases often end in death.

Damage to the facial nerve

The nervous supply to the front of the face, including the lips and nostrils, comes from one nerve, the facial nerve. This nerve runs along the side of the mouth. Kicks, blows and severe kinds of bridles on the cheeks can all damage the nerve. If the cheeks get pierced or crushed, signs of paralysis may appear. The nostrils and the lower lip will hang slack. Crushed nerves can regenerate again. If the nerve is severed, the nerve endings will renew again after a few days or weeks. Permanent paralysis of the facial nerve does not often happen.

Diseases of the salivary glands

The ducts of the salivary glands are very superficial. Outside injuries will quickly cause damage. The duct of the parotid gland starts off deep and then becomes superficial where it joins the blood vessels and nerves to wrap around the bone of the lower jaw with just the skin protecting it. This is the spot where the pulse of the horse can be taken. With injury the nerves, blood vessels and the duct of the salivary gland get damaged. The parotid salivary gland produces 50 milliliters of saliva per minute. When the duct is opened due to injury, it is important to surgically seal it. There is no danger of infection, for the saliva has the function of both cleansing and disinfecting.

Injuries to the cheeks can also cause damage to the salivary ducts. In favorable situations the duct will heal perfectly without surgical intervention, but otherwise, a fistula appears, where the saliva will permanently drip out.

The fistula can heal with localized treatment, but it is better to surgically seal it.

Horses seldom have stones in their salivary duct, although this is possible when foreign bodies sometimes penetrate the openings of the salivary ducts.

The foreign bodies are mainly wood splinters or grass stems, with limestone building up around it, much the same as with tartar build-up around the teeth. This obstructs the flow of saliva and results in an infection in the area of the stone. The end of the salivary duct swells and is painful to touch. The glands should be opened under general anaesthetic, rinsed and carefully stitched again.

The salivary glands have a secondary function in the lymphatic system. The salivary glands can swell up when a horse eats certain plants which provoke an allergic reaction. This is often the case with the parotid gland that shows an obvious swelling in the pasture season. This is the season when the grasses are in flower and many horses exhibit an allergic reaction to that. Once the flowering season has passed, the swelling of the glands will go down again. The rideability of the horse is impaired at this time. When the horse works on the bit, the swelling that takes place in the parotid gland prevents the closed angle between the head and neck. The counterpressure against the swollen salivary duct is painful, and the horse will resist the compression. Medication will only serve to moderate the symptoms; keeping the horse in the stable and feeding it hay will get rid of the cause.

Other diseases

The same symptoms as described above can be caused by disease of the pharynx, larynx and top portion of the esophagus. Expanding into that, however, is beyond the scope of this book.

The objective of this book is not to make a veterinarian of every reader; rather, it is intended to assist the reader in the detection of diseases at an early stage, so that they can be treated accordingly.

Examination of the Teeth and Mouth – When, How and Why?

5

When is an examination of the teeth and mouth necessary?

The end result and incidence of tooth-related disease are often underestimated. Many problems are not initially considered as tooth-related. Back problems, recurring blockage of the esophagus and colics are but a few diseases that can be associated with problems of the teeth. Regular examination of the mouth and in particular the teeth can make it easier to prevent problems by identifying them early.

The general impression of the horse must be taken into account when there is any suspicion of disease from the teeth. Skinny horses or horses with a dull coat are definitely candidates for a tooth-related disease. The feeding, level of work and possible parasitic infection of the horse should also be considered in a case like this. If whole grains and undigested food are found in the droppings of the horse, the suspicion becomes certainty that the problem is connected to the teeth. Lethargic horses that have no appetite and perform below their abilities may also have tooth-associated problems. Specific diseases have already been discussed.

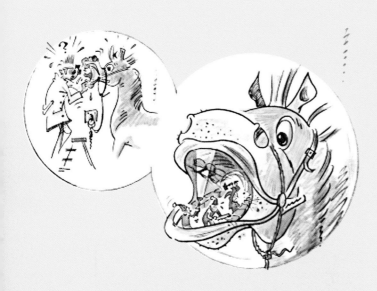

At what age do horses have problems with their teeth?

"My horse is only five – he cannot have anything wrong with his teeth!"

"In the olden days you only started to look in the horse's mouth when he was ten!"

Such attitudes provoke daily arguments with horse owners. These opinions, however, are outdated. As long ago as the 1920s, veterinarians had started to develop their own instruments for the treatment of horses' teeth, and cavalry horses had regular dental examinations. Nevertheless, care of the teeth has hitherto been somewhat neglected. Sophisticated treatments like endoscopies, ultrasound, X-rays and many more were given higher value. Simple matters, for instance the examination of teeth, were only considered as an afterthought. This has now changed completely, and much more thought is given to the significance of the teeth. There are specific problems with the mouth and teeth at all stages of the horse's life, and these will be discussed next.

The foal

The foal has the central incisors and first premolars present as milk teeth when born. The completeness of the mouth can be ascertained at this young age. Incorrect jaw positions can be corrected at a young age, when recognized early enough. This includes the shorter lower jaw of the parrot mouth and the too long lower jaw of the pig mouth (sometimes also called monkey mouth). Twisted upper jaws, splits in the jaw and incomplete gingiva are all problems that can be treated when observed early. The split in the palate is revealed when the foal suckles, and the milk runs out of the nostrils.

The two-year-old horse

It is important at this age to check that the horse has all the teeth that it should have, or that they are at least busy erupting in the mouth. The premolars must be checked for sharp edges as well. At this age the horses have a growth spurt, and optimum feeding is necessary. When they do not eat enough or do not grind their food properly, it can have a negative influence on their development.

The three- to four-year-old horse

Some of the horses in this age group are already being used intensely as riding horses. Between the ages of two and a half to four and a half, the young horse will shed all 24 of its milk teeth.

The horse in this photo is three and a half years old. The intermediate incisor in the upper jaw is pushing the milk tooth out. In the lower jaw the intermediate incisor is fully erupted. Both the corner incisors are still milk teeth.

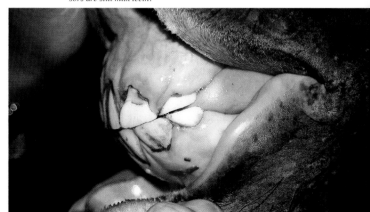

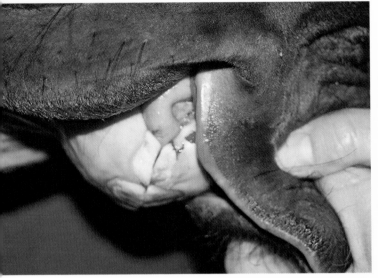

This horse is five years old. The corner incisor has been shed but is not yet in occlusion.

Depending on the horse, 36 to 44 permanent teeth are formed. Feeding and riding can be intensely influenced by the changes taking place in the jawbone, gums, hard and soft parts of the socket and the delayed loss of the caps of milk teeth. Retained caps and the socket of the primary tooth can cause the jawbone to swell. Sharp edges on the teeth and caps will irritate the cheeks and tongue. Retained caps on the premolars of one side of the mouth will cause uneven wear on the molars in the other side of the mouth.

When the development of the incisors is delayed, the horizontal surface of the incisors is changed, and that may hinder the mobility of the lower jaw. This is also the time where the wolf teeth develop, and riding of the young horses can be obstructed due to the pain caused by the unerupted or hidden wolf tooth. Stallions and geldings have a second helping of this when the canines develop in the fourth year.

Unfortunately not all canines develop without drama. Some of them remain below gum level, and the bulge formed can be extremely painful. Molars that grow at an angle will influence the chewing ability of the horse.

This is the most vulnerable age as far as teeth are concerned, and problems are more likely to occur at this time. It is of utmost importance to examine the teeth at least twice yearly at this age.

The five- to ten-year-old horse

Horses of this age have a full set of permanent teeth. They are mostly ridden, and problems with shedding are not expected anymore.

This horse is ten years old. The corner incisor is as long as it is wide.

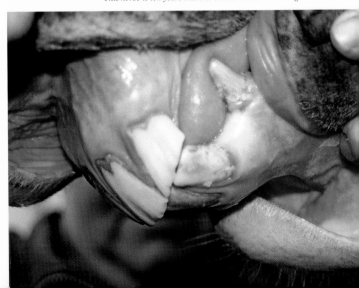

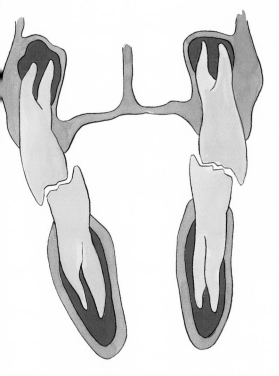

The sideways movement of the lower jaw against the upper jaw is obstructed due to the formation of hooks.

develop at different rates, the grinding of food can be insufficient due to too long incisors or too much wear on the molars. This can be checked by the amount of sideways movement of the lower jaw against the upper jaw; the lower jaw should be displaced by about a half of the breadth of an incisor and show a definite contact on the molars with further pressure. If the pressure rises even more with the sideways movement of the lower jaw, the slit of the mouth will open slowly. The molars will grind on each other, and because of the 10-15 degree slant in the teeth, the lower jaw will be displaced down. If this is not possible, there is something amiss in the area of the molars.

Seven- to ten-year-old horses develop a hook in the upper corner incisor; this may affect the mobility of the lower jaw in the ridden horse.

A yearly examination is sufficient when the teeth have a normal position.

The reserve crown (under the gum line) develops until the eighth year and grows into the space of the jawbone. It is quite possible for the horse to have a painful reaction due to the pressures of the developing teeth. Insufficient wear on the chewing surfaces will now become apparent. Hooks and ramps are often the culprits.

The canine teeth in stallions and geldings (and some mares) frequently mature into big, sharp teeth. Remember, they used to be utilized as a weapon!

Uniform contact of the teeth is very important at this age. The incisors as well as the molars should be in matching occlusion. If the incisors and molars

The ten- to eighteen-year-old horse

Uneven wear and incorrect positioning of the teeth are the biggest problems at this age. The pressure exerted through uneven wear can cause spontaneous fracturing and inflammation of the socket of the tooth. The teeth that suffer the most from the uneven wear are the first premolars of the upper jaw.

The first premolars of the upper and lower jaw develop an uneven proportion of length to each other. When this is recognized at an early enough stage, it can be corrected.

The uneven share of pressure will become apparent on the incisors. The angle of the incisors of the

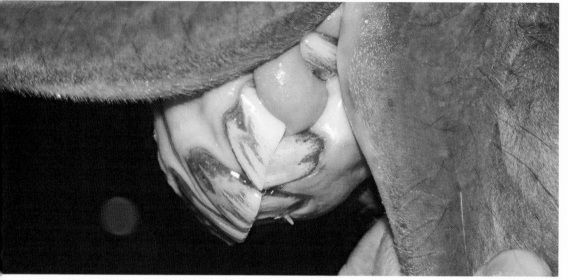

This horse is thirteen years old. The groove on the corner incisor is halfway down the length of the tooth.

lower jaw becomes slanted, while the angle of the incisors of the upper jaw stays upright for a while longer. This means the wear on the incisors of the upper jaw is more on the back of the chewing surface, and the wear of the incisors of the lower jaw is more on the front of the chewing surface. The hooks that form on the upper premolar will encourage this situation; the result is that the incisors of the lower jaw and the lower jaw itself will be pushed back, putting incredible pressure on the jaw joint. The amount the lower jaw moves to the front when the horse is ridden on the bit is insignificant. This mechanism will be prevented by the slanted wear of the chewing surfaces on the incisors. Problems with riding are in store!

The slanted incisors, the hook on the premolar and the backwards movement of the lower jaw are accelerated. In extreme cases the chewing surfaces of the incisors do not come into contact with each other, which means there will be no wear taking place. The incisors become longer, and influence the function of the molars. The molars do not grind the food properly, the digestibility of the food is lowered, and the horse loses weight without any obvious reason. Early correction can prevent this from happening.

Canines can also be a problem at this age. They can be extremely sharp and then cut the tongue of the horse and even the hand of the person examining the mouth. The bit in the mouth of the horse causes the tongue to bulge to the front and the back of the bit. The front part of the tongue lies between the canine teeth, and the sharpness of the teeth can cause considerable discomfort when the horse is ridden.

Eighteen years and older

Old horses often have problems with wear of the teeth. Incorrect positioning and irregular wear of the teeth increase with age.

Hooks and ramps on the molars are almost always found in the older horse. The little remaining tooth substance found in the old horse due to the wear of years is very unstable. The possibility of fractures and infection of the socket increases. The older the horse, the more loose teeth will be found that will not necessarily fall out by themselves. The sockets of these teeth are prone to infection due to the ease with which food particles can get stuck in them. Identification of the loose teeth will prevent infection.

This horse is very old, for the teeth are protruding well to the front. It is impossible to age the horse correctly due to these projecting teeth.

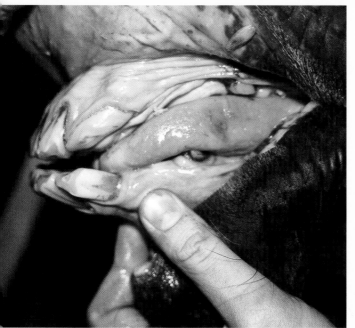

Old horses wear their teeth down to the root. After the transition between crown and root, there is no more hard substance of enamel. The root consists only of softer dentine and cementum. The old tooth will therefore be worn away within a short period of time. It is therefore recommended to have a twice-yearly dental examination done on old horses.

How is the examination of teeth and mouth carried out?

Examination of the mouth and teeth is not limited to the structures inside the mouth, but includes everything connected to the mechanics of chewing and the outer contours of the head.

The examination should commence with a scrutiny of the head. Under normal circumstances the left- and right-hand sides of the head are symmetrical. Any swelling and dissimilar structures will immediately be noticed upon inspection of the head.

The examination should start with palpation of the head, taking the anatomy into consideration. The palpation must be done comparing the two sides with each other. Start at the base of the ear, searching for swellings or crustiness of the skin.

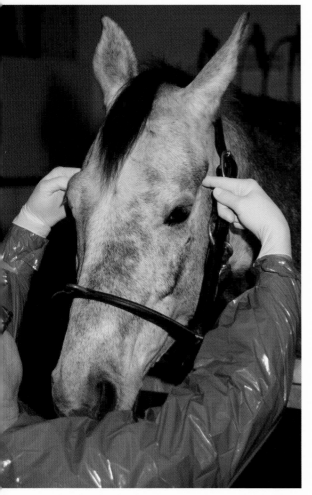

It is best to examine the jaw joints simultaneously on both sides of the face. This way any irregularities can be detected.

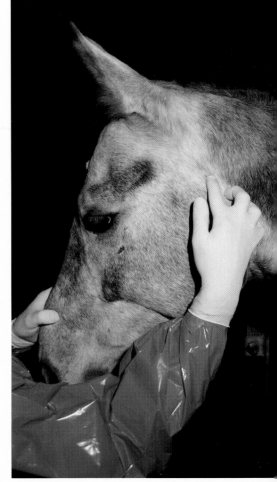

The parotid is the biggest salivary gland in the horse.

The next point is behind the eye, in the area of the jaw joint. If the horse shows a reaction to pressure on this joint, it is possibly a sign of trouble with the mechanics of chewing.

The most practical way is to follow the bone of the jaw and check for any swellings, painful areas and erratic structures. Soft tissue structures such as the parotid salivary gland should also be given an assessment when it comes to problems with

riding. The parotid gland lies under the branches of the lower jaw, and sufficient freedom for the jowl is often a problem even in the healthy horse. When the horse works on the bit, the jowl is closer to the neck; the space is much less than when at rest, and this causes pressure on the parotid gland, which the horse will try and evade. The pressure is lessened when saliva is excreted, but in individual cases this might not be enough.

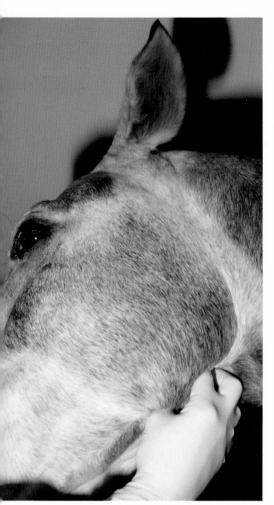

The lymph nodes can be found between the branches of the lower jaw. They serve large parts of the mouth and teeth. This area must be checked for swelling and pain.

for alarm. If, however, the horse reacts violently and an asymmetric swelling can be felt, this can indicate inflammation in the area of the teeth.

Following the line of the jaw towards the mouth, the mandibular salivary gland is felt between the branches of the jaw. The only time these will swell is when there are stones in the saliva. The jawbone of the young horse, three to five years old, will have bumps from the developing teeth. Young horses can, as is the case with young children, react sensitively when shedding teeth, and development of the permanent teeth can limit their quality of performance.

Palpation of the upper jaw, likewise, will reveal any swellings and pain in the areas of the sinuses and the teeth. Knocking against the area of the sinus with the knuckle will bring forth spontaneous defensive reactions from the horse if some discomfort is present. The hollow sound that is normal when knocking on the sinuses will be more muffled.

These horses have problems with working in an outline.

Two structures of different sizes will sometimes be found between the branches of the jaw. These are the lymph nodes of the lower jaw, and they will react to inflammation of any kind. If the consistency of the node is soft and the horse does not over-react with soft pressure, there should be no cause

Reactions within the jawbone come from the development of the permanent teeth. They are called bumps and can be painful when touched.

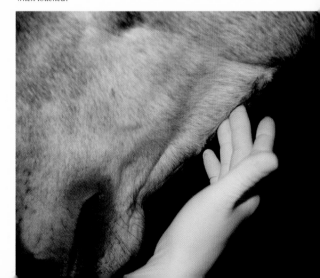

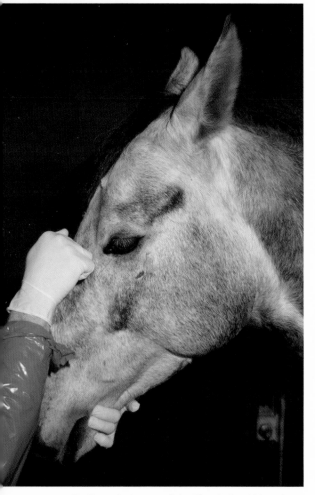

Knocking on the sinuses can distinguish a raised sensitivity or change in the sound due to filling with liquid.

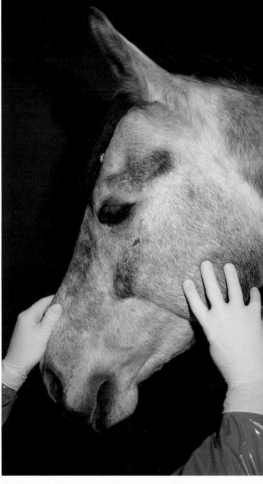

Swelling, painful areas and hardened sections of the chewing muscles can be found by light palpation.

This points to filling of the sinuses and a patho-logical process. The difference in the noise must always be compared to that of the other side.

The most important area on the horse's head is the region containing the rows of molars. Light pal-pation here will reveal painful reactions, swelling and even any loose teeth. This gives a reasonably good impression of what is to be found on the inside of the mouth, which is otherwise difficult to exam-ine without the correct equipment.

It is recommended to do a functional test in this area. Hold the horse's nose on the bridge with one hand and move the lower jaw sideways with the other hand.

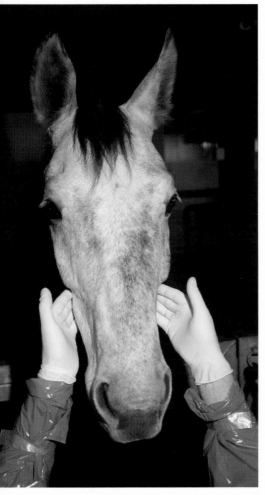

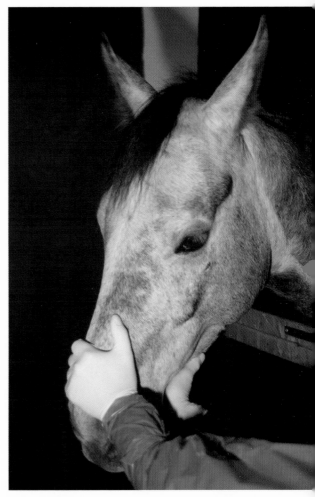

Palpation of the cheeks can point to changes in the mouth that will normally only be found using special tools.

Holding in place the upper jaw with one hand and moving the lower jaw against the upper jaw with the other hand will test if there is something wrong with the mechanics of chewing.

Under normal circumstances, the lower jaw can easily be moved side to side by approximately the breadth of half an incisor. The molars will then come into contact and with increased pressure the movement can be continued. While doing this, the slit of the mouth will open, depending on the angle of the molars.

This test should be done to both sides. If the sideways movement cannot be done in one direction, it may be that the molars have hooks or ramps.

Examining the lips and the bars of the mouth should be part of the routine. There are often injuries and embedded grasses or other foreign bodies in the lips. The lips and bars of the mouth are extremely sensitive, and small defects can clearly have an

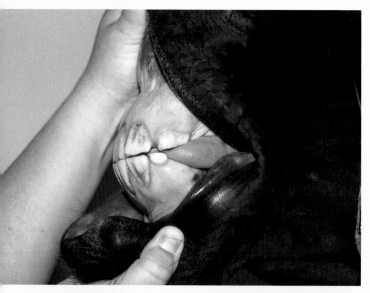

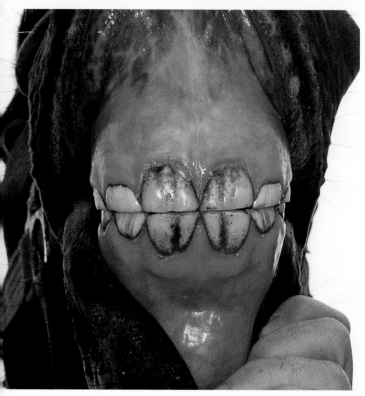

The incisors should first be examined with the surfaces touching. The examination should be done from the side and the front. The teeth should be judged according to how well they fit the opposing teeth.

immense effect on the feeding and ride-ability of the horse.

In the course of inspecting the lips, the examination of the inside of the mouth has already begun. Opening the lips exposes the incisors, and the way the two jaws stand in relation to each other can be assessed. Ideally the upper and lower incisors should fit exactly, from the front as well as the side. Many horses have a minor underbite, where the lower jaw is slightly shorter than the upper jaw. Some-times the lower jaw can be a little to one side. This might mean the molars are worn down more on one side, pushing the lower jaw to one side.

The slit in the mouth can be opened by moderate pressure on the lower jaw. Fractured and worn teeth can be easily identified. Horses that crib-bite, where they bite into hard objects such as the feeding trough and then swallow air, almost invariably have extreme wear on the front of the incisors of the upper jaw. This is not always just a sign of crib-bit-ing; some horses will drag their teeth along the metal bars that divide the sta-bles, out of pure boredom.

These horses will also have upper inci-sors that are more worn than is usual.

Young horses that are shedding their teeth will frequently have the cap of the milk tooth retained on the permanent tooth. This might hinder the complete eruption of the permanent tooth. In extreme cases the milk tooth and the permanent tooth form a double row. The permanent tooth erupts behind the deciduous tooth, and there are often too many teeth that stay put in this situation.

In the examination of the horse all the senses should be utilized. Under normal circumstances, the breath of the horse is quite aromatic: the breath of plant-eaters is much more pleasant than that of meat-eaters. Infection in the mouth, especially infection of the teeth, however, will cause a characteristic bad smell from the mouth. This smell is foul and penetrating, like the smell of eggs gone bad. Once smelled, it is never forgotten! This is why the sense of smell should be part of the evaluation.

The canines are in the interdental space, behind the incisors. These teeth can be extremely sharp in older stallions, geldings and the occasional mare. The roots of these teeth are very long and lie bent to the back of the jaw.

Unerupted canines are much more of a problem. They stay just below the level of the gum and are sensitive when touched. The inspection of the interdental space is an important checkpoint. Further to the back of the mouth are the premolars.

Sometimes there will be a small and insignificant little tooth in front of the first "real" premolar. This is the wolf tooth. Why this tooth is called the wolf tooth is not clear. In the tooth formula this little tooth is present as a regular premolar (P1). However, it

The horse's breath must be checked. A foul smell will mean an inflammation is present.

Inspection of the interdental space is an important part of the examination.

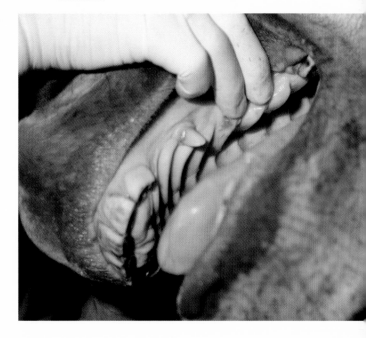

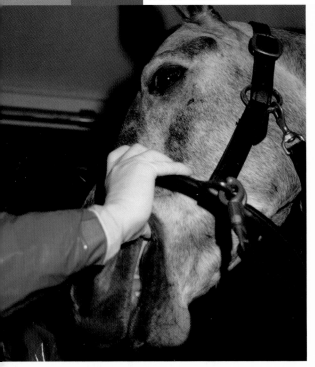

It is important to establish whether a wolf tooth is present. A sensitive reaction to finger pressure is a sign of a hidden wolf tooth.

The soft tissue of the mouth, the mucous membranes, gums and tongue must also be checked.

is only a remnant tooth with a little root. As is the case with the canine, the wolf tooth can also be hidden, remaining just under the level of the gum. Light pressure with painful reactions can show the exact location of the hidden wolf tooth. The wolf tooth is almost exclusively found in the upper jaw, but it is not impossible to find one in the lower jaw. The wolf tooth can also erupt out of the line of the other teeth. In the examination of the interdental space, the area of the lips and bars of the mouth as well as to the tongue must be checked for scattered teeth. It is possible to sometimes find these little teeth even under

the tongue. It is quite understandable that horses will resist being ridden when the area where the bit goes is painful.

Examination of the premolars and molars is not without difficulty. The first premolar can be reached with relative ease. A slight underbite will regularly imply a hook formed on the front of the first premolar of the upper jaw. Sharp edges on the outside of the tooth in the upper jaw and on the inside of the tooth in the lower jaw will frequently be found as well.

Caps from milk teeth are not often found on the

first premolar. The caps will more often than not tilt and become wedged between two neighboring teeth. The first premolar has no neighbor so there will be no caps caught here.

The mucous membranes and the tongue must be incorporated in the examination of the mouth, noting injuries and inflammation.

The second premolar requires more experience and courage from the person doing the examination. Ramps can be found on the outside of the upper teeth and on the inside of the lower teeth as well as the retained caps from the milk teeth. The milk teeth caps will sometimes tilt and get caught between the first and third permanent premolars, possibly causing inflammation of the tongue or mucous membrane.

Examining the third premolar is not for the faint-hearted. Ramps and caps will be found here as above. Fractured and loose premolars may also be found in older horses.

The molars are the most difficult teeth of all to examine. To try to do so without the correct equipment, for example the mouth speculum, is madness. Many have made acquaintance with the power of the chewing muscle, losing a fingernail in the process.

It is possible to see quite far into the mouth with the help of a good headlamp. This is only likely if the horse has its mouth wide open. A dentist would ask the patient to say "ah." This unfortunately does not work with the horse, but there are a few tricks to open the mouth, and they will be described below.

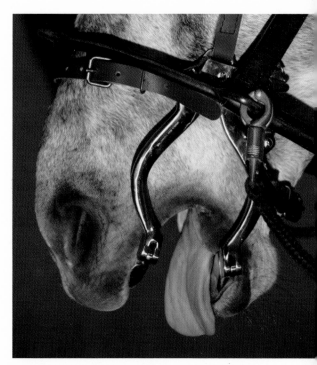

Examination of the back of the mouth is only possible with the help of a mouth speculum.

A good source of light will make the examination easier.

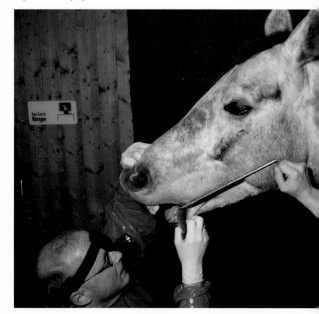

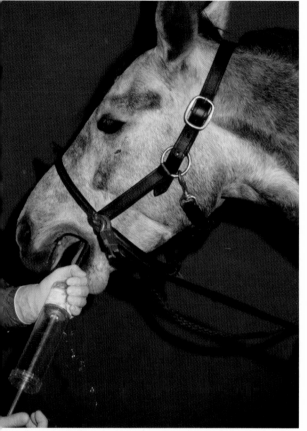

Get rid of food particles in the mouth by rinsing it out.

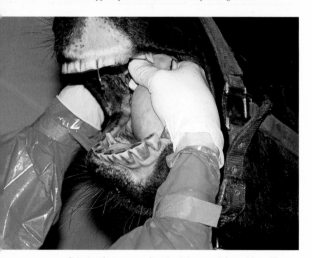

Gripping the tongue and putting it in an upright position will open the mouth without the help of any tools. A good source of light is absolutely necessary when opening the mouth this way.

Horses with tooth problems will often have food rests in their cheeks. Food rests in the mouths of healthy horses can complicate the task of examining the mouth. Rinsing the horse's mouth to clear away all the bits will help. Many horses like it when the mouth is bathed with a hose, but for those who are not as enthusiastic, a big syringe can be used to spray into the side of the mouth.

It is possible to open the horse's mouth without the use of equipment, using the hand to grip the tongue. Take care! The horse's tongue may be relatively long, but it is only attached to the floor of the mouth by a thin layer of soft tissue. This fragile connection can easily be torn if too much force is used. The next step when the tongue is gripped is to try and put it in an upright position. The horse does not want to bite its own tongue and will therefore open its mouth. The bars of the mouth can then be pulled away, and with the help of a headlamp, one side of the molars can be inspected.

Aside from the sharp ramps, irritation of the cheek and tongue, fractured or incorrect teeth, the molars right at the back of the mouth must also be examined. Many horses have a slight underbite and this means the edge of the last molar in the lower jaw will not be sufficiently worn. The chewing surfaces of the molars curve upwards according to the upward slant of the jawbones. In horses with short heads it is therefore not easy to inspect the teeth with the headlamp alone. Occasionally there will be an extra molar behind the third molar (M3). The shorter and more slanted the jawbone, the more difficult it will be to assess the tooth at the back, or if any extra teeth are at hand. This situation calls for specialized equipment.

Mouth speculums, gags or wedges are available for these circumstances. These aids should be handled with care, for horses that have not been sedated might react in an unpredictable way. Even the most well-behaved horse does not necessarily get a mouth gag or speculum in its mouth as a daily routine. According to the experience of a friendly dentist, the most good-natured people are often the most difficult in the dental chair. It is frequently the case with horses too!

Placing the mouth wedge in the horse's mouth should be done with great care. Doing so requires knowledge of the anatomy of the horse's head. The wedge must be placed between the upper and lower rows of the molars, and the mouth must be well opened to do this. If the wedge slips off the row of teeth it can hurt the cheeks of the horse, and the odds are that it would become dangerous for the person doing the examination. If the wedge slips to the inside of the mouth, the palate can be injured. There is a relatively big blood vessel in the palate and it can cause excessive bleeding when the palate gets injured. The amount of blood, mixed with saliva, can be dramatic, making everybody nervous. Placing the wedge in the mouth should be a matter of course in an examination. Most wedges have a rope to cross behind the ears, and a helper can hold this or tie it onto the head collar.

The tools used for the examination will be described on page 108ff. The mouth can now be inspected by hand. Palpation of the upper and lower rows of teeth can reveal irregularities, and the following questions can also be answered:

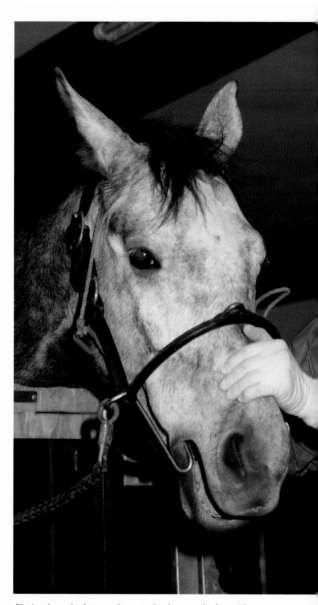

Placing the wedge between the rows of molars must be done with the help of an assistant.

- Are the teeth correctly aligned in a single row?
- Are there spaces between the single teeth?
- Are all the teeth worn down equally?
- Are there any hooks or ramps on the teeth?
- Are there any fractured or missing teeth?
- Are there more than six molars?
- Is the last tooth on the same level as the rest of the chewing surface?
- Does the horse's breath smell?
- Are there any soft tissue changes or injuries on the mucous membranes or tongue?

How do I restrain my horse?

Having to undergo an examination of its mouth is an unfamiliar experience and not always enjoyable for the horse. In comparison to humans, the horse is tremendously powerful and can defend itself very effectively against unpleasant events. The potential danger to both the horse and the people around it

Not all horses cooperate in the dental examination.

must not be underestimated. Horses are animals of flight, and this is the first thing they will attempt to do when they feel threatened, frightened or have pain inflicted upon them. The direction of flight in the examination of teeth is normally backwards. The stabled horse, whose natural direction of flight is blocked, can react in an unpredictable way by "fleeing" forwards. This could be pushing forward, rearing or a combination of the two. The threat to the people around the horse is magnified. This is a good enough reason to reduce the pain and reflex situation for the horse, and there are various techniques of doing this.

Manual procedures for appropriate handling of the horse

Picking up a leg as a measure of discipline should only be used when the horse does not stand still. This is seldom necessary for the dental examination, mostly because it is not really effective.

The skin-hold is a surprisingly effective way of restraining a horse. Simply take a "handful" of skin on the neck and hold it to make a bulge. The same receptors are triggered that make the nose twitch work. This could have a calming or painful influence, depending on the type of horse. Horses do not take exception to these measures either.

If a horse is difficult, it is not suggested that the tongue gets pulled out as a disciplining measure. This was a "trick" used by horse traders and blacksmiths in the olden days.

The skin-hold is an effective way to pacify a horse.

The same pain-reducing mechanism is not applicable as with the nose twitch, and the effectiveness of the calming is also negative. The inspection of the mouth becomes a traumatic situation attended by a real danger of injury to the tongue.

Qualified specialists in the field may apply acupuncture and acupressure as possible methods of placating the horse. More detailed information will be discussed below.

Aids to restrain the horse

Many horse lovers habitually regard the nose twitch as an instrument of torture. The twitch is utilized in certain circumstances to pacify the horse as a matter of course and is made of a 20-30 centimeter long wooden handle with a loop of hemp at the end. This loop is twisted around the lip with the wooden handle; this can be twisted tightly or loosely. There are also loops made of chains or rope and twitches made of metal on the market.

The nose twitch is and was an unpopular means of coercion to calm horses. They should only be employed in short intervals, for example with the dental examination, the blacksmith or when clipping the horse. For many horse owners this is not a pleasant sight, and for the horse it probably is accompanied by considerable pain. The accompanying pain has been mentioned in literature from way back. The horse dictionary of Count von Norman (1939) called the twitch a "cruel instrument of torture … a rope twisted around the top lip of a horse with a wooden handle to force it to stand still, especially for the blacksmith." In the horse and rider dictionary of Jasper Nissen (1976), the twitch is described as a method of coercion that causes so much pain that the horse's awareness is distracted.

The latest findings show that the use of the nose twitch and the irritation it causes to the tissues will cause the release of endorphins. Endorphins are opiate-like substances and are strongly analgesic painkillers, reducing the sensation of pain. The triggering of a certain part of the brain releases endorphins into the blood and a short-term anesthetic is achieved. This is the body's own morphine. It is believed that opiates increase the horse's pain threshold. Endorphins are also released in acupuncture and acupressure. It is thought that the twitch on the nose triggers such an acupuncture or acupressure point.

Triggering of acupuncture points is also an argument in the ear and skin-hold. Holding the ear as a means of twitch is not recommended, for the elimination of pain is unsatisfactory in this case.

The main result from holding the ear with undue force is that the horse becomes ear-shy, and that can

The nose twitch is traditionally used to restrain unmanageable horses. The twitch has a long handle, allowing the person using it to be well out of harm's way.

hardly be what is intended. The skin-hold is a very successful way of calming the horse, but is inferior to the twitch, which remains the easiest and most effective way to calm a horse for short periods of time in different situations. It should not be applied for longer than 15-20 minutes at any time. The metal twitches are especially severe, with a greater danger of damaging the soft tissue. Care must be taken that the twitch is not put on too high, and in the process closing one or both nostrils. The twitch should only be used as a last resort and then only used sparingly.

If the horse reacts so violently that the safety of the handler, examiner and the horse itself is at risk, the use of the twitch may become essential. Many horse owners are reluctant to use the twitch on their horses, but they forget that the horse is indirectly a danger to itself and the twitch acts as a means of protection.

In some cases the twitch is twisted too tight, which then brings on a violent reaction from the horse. If the twist is slackened, the horse will usually calm down again. There are, however, horses for which the twitch will not have the desired calming effect. The twitch should therefore not always be employed regardless. In some cases it is prudent to give the horse a sedating drug in order to avoid unnecessary agitation and not completing the examination.

From personal experience I recommend a twitch with a thick hemp loop and a long handle, about 80 centimeters long. The handler will be able to keep a good distance to the side of the horse, keeping clear from the front legs if the horse stamps or leaps forward. If the handle is too short, this can be a certain danger to the assistant.

In the hand of an expert, the twitch is an acceptable technique to restrain horses with short and effective application when and where necessary. To say the horse is being tortured with the twitch is not always true. On the other hand, its use requires care so that it is not harmful to the horse. In the hands of an experienced person the twitch is a practical support to minimize the risk of injury for all the people involved as well as the horse.

By far the must suitable way to carry out a dental examination, however, is to have the horse in a crush. This will allow even an inexperienced person to inspect the horse's mouth with reduced risk. The horse stands in a metal or wooden construction that is fixed to the ground and is completely enclosed with a door or pole in the front and back. In this situation it is also possible to tie up the horse properly. Horses that do not travel well in trailers might get claustrophobic when they have to stand in a crush, and it is better to sedate these horses.

The crush is a safe location for both the horse and handler to participate in a dental examination.

Calming the horse with sedatives

Sedating pharmaceuticals are divided into tranquilizers and sedatives.

Tranquilisers are central calming substances and are mostly used when the horse moves into new stables or similar events, when the blacksmith comes and also when dental examinations are being performed on really difficult animals. Acetylpromazin is the standard tranquilizer used.

After administration of the drug, the animals are composed, uninterested and unconcerned but still fully conscious. This drug is administrated in veterinary examinations, during slightly painful interventions and to pacify easily excitable or unmanageable horses.

All the above administrations are so-called "inside jobs," where the drug is given in small doses, the objective being to calm the excitable horse to

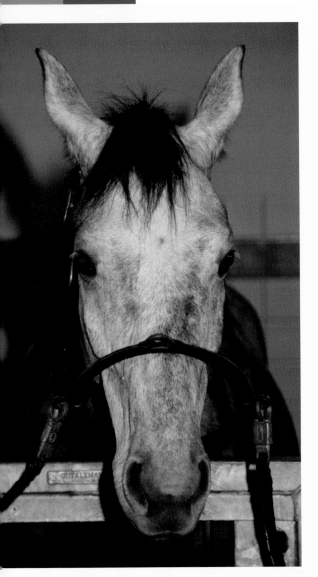

In order to make the dental examination easier, this horse has been sedated.

become more manageable. The effect of the drug lasts for about six hours, which will leave ample time to do the examination on the horse's mouth.

The most used of the group known as sedatives are the so-called alpha-2-agonists. These can induce sedation (calming), general anaesthesia (not receptive to pain), and muscle relaxation. The effect depends on the doses and the method of administration (intravenous – in the blood vessel, or intramuscular). The period of effectiveness for the sedatives is considerably shorter than for acetylpromazin, and can be anything from one to two hours. The ability to stand is obviously affected by the muscle-relaxing action, which means the doses cannot be changed at will. Increasing the doses can have side-effects on the heart and lungs. Intravenous administration will be effective within four minutes, making it a fast and effective technique to pacify horses. The horse is relaxed, and the dental examination can be performed without resistance.

The effect lasts for at least 20 minutes and decreases slowly within the next 60 minutes. The alpha-2-agonists are not suitable for top-up sedation to achieve a longer period of calming.

Horses should preferably not eat for two hours after being sedated: the reduction of the reflex to swallow can give rise to blockages of the pharynx.

There are also alternative medications available for horses that are not as excitable, including homeopathic treatment as well as plant extracts.

Alternative treatment: Holistic veterinary care for teeth problems

(By Dr. Sabine Gajdoss, Veterinarian)

The question: "Can regular dental examination be replaced by holistic medicine?" can only be answered with a "No." However, if the question is: "Can the treatment of teeth be made more bearable by administering holistic remedies?" the answer to that has to be a clear "Yes."

The more knowledge the specialist in his or her field has, the more affirmative the answer to the above question. It is possible, however, for the layperson to make the procedure stress-free for their horse.

Just as in humans, horses are born with the eventual construction and positioning of their teeth genetically predetermined. This cannot be influenced by holistic methods.

Holistic medicine can definitely influence the healing of wounds when teeth are extracted and of abscesses that are formed in the mucous membranes, as well as all kinds of corrections that are not necessarily pleasant for the horse.

The quantity of holistic treatments available is so infinite that their inclusion would make this book burst at the seams. However, all of these methods have one thing in common: they consider the whole patient, including their environment and history. The focus of any holistic treatment should always be the horse, not the abscess or the toothache.

At this point a few opinions can be offered. For those of you who would like to know more, reading the extended book list at the end of this chapter is offered.

Specialist acupuncturists and homeopaths are recommended for those who would like to have their horses treated using holistic methods. The American Association of Equine Practitioners has the names available of veterinarians who also specialize in holistic therapies. The veterinarian that treats your stable may furthermore know of or practice holistic methods or may be able to refer you to someone who does.

Four areas of holistic therapy have been chosen and will be dealt with:
• acupressure
• homeopathy
• Bach flower remedies
• phytotherapy.

The idea is to speed up the healing of the damage done to the body, to calm the horse down and to minimize the emotional burden of the treatment.

Acupressure

Acupressure is one of the oldest methods of healing, if not the oldest. Traditional Chinese medicine and acupuncture originate from the knowledge of acupressure. The philosophy behind the choice of points and the type of treatment is incredibly complex but logical.

Acupressure treatment is the application of pressure at specific points. Tension can be relieved; imbalances can be addressed, and potential weak points can be strengthened. One or more fingers and even the whole hand can be utilized in acupressure. The most suitable way is the method of balancing.

The chosen point is carefully touched, and then the whole hand takes up the contact, increasing the pressure in clockwise circles. When the animal shows signs of relaxation, the optimum pressure for "this point on this horse" has been reached. The mouth relaxes, the ears flop slightly, the eyes become soft and the eyelids start to close.

Unfortunately it is not possible to achieve this kind of relaxation when someone is busy working with an electrical rotary file on the horse's teeth.

Objective preparation through acupressure, which can be repeated from time to time during the treatment of the teeth, can settle the horse down and help it to deal better with the course of events. There are various points where the horse reacts well:

- One point lies on the forehead of the horse, on the midline just above the eyes. If a line is drawn from the corner of the inside of the right eye to the base of the left ear and a second line from the corner of the inside of the left eye to the base of the right ear, the point lies where the two lines cross.
- A second point lies on the midline where a horizontal line from the lower border of the nostrils crosses the midline.
- The third point on the midline is on the lower jaw in the hollow where the smooth skin goes over into hairy skin.

In order to relax the horse, these points should be massaged, using circular movements, in the above

Accupressure to the head helps to settle nervous horses.

order. The first point is treated for 60 seconds and the next two for 30 seconds each.

Points of the eye

There are many important points around the eye that can be used in standard acupressure. According to the traditional Chinese medicine, many body meridians and the so-called extraordinary meridians meet in and around the eye. This is the reason why massage in this area can be very calming and balancing for the horse.

Starting on the inside corner of the eye, the lower edge of the eye socket is massaged all the way around to the outside corner of the eye, then along the upper eyelid on the edge of the socket of the eye back to the inside corner. This can be done using the whole hand or single fingers, depending on what the horse prefers.

There are several other points that can add to the soothing of the horse. If you want to know more on this topic, you should get in touch with a specialist in this subject or read from the suggested booklist.

Homeopathy

In the early nineteenth century, Dr. Samuel Hahneman developed what is still known as homeopathy. The fundamental basis of this philosophy is that "like heals like." Homeopathy, like acupressure, is a specialized field. The whole horse is included in the diagnosis, and, as is the case with acupressure, there is no remedy for toothache. There are, however, numerous preparations to treat the symptoms. Here are some examples.

Arnica Montana (leopard's bane, arnica)

Arnica is a most important remedy when it comes to fresh wounds that bleed, injuries, bruises that are painful when touched, post-operative conditions and weakness through loss of blood. The best treatment is 15 tablets or 15-20 drops of the dilution of the potency D 6. The remedy is administered until healing has commenced.

Symphytum (comfrey)

What arnica is to soft tissue, comfrey is to bone. It is beneficial for all injuries to bone, cartilage and the periosteum (thin layer that covers bone) and after extraction of a tooth. Administer 15 tablets or 15-20 drops of the dilution of the potency D 6.

Hamamelis (witch hazel)

Witch hazel is used for venous bleeding, injuries that ooze blood, contusions with hematomas that immediately turn blue, old hematomas and older and pale animals.

Administer 15 tablets or 15-20 drops of the dilution of potency D 6.

Calendula (pot marigold)

In contrast to the above-mentioned remedies, pot marigold is only used externally and in tincture form (D 2). It promotes the formation of connective tissue and acts as a disinfectant. The tincture can be used to rinse the wound after extraction of a tooth.

These few remedies represent only a very small part of homeopathy and the healing effect it has. They should only be administered on the prescription of the veterinarian or homeopath. There is no problem administering homeopathic remedies in conjunction with conventional medicine, for the very low strength of the highly diluted preparations means that they are incapable of causing any interference.

Phytotherapy

Treatment using plants, parts of plants, extracts of plants or natural products can be described as phytotherapy; this means anything described under the heading of medicinal herbs.

There are many ways to prepare these medicinal herbs. The easiest is tea, which, when cooled off, can be poured over the feed. Many herbs can also be fed fresh or dried.

Here are a few pacifying herbs that are becoming ever more popular in their healing capacities.

Matricaria recutita (German chamomile)

The flowers of the chamomile plant are calming, anti-inflammatory, relaxing and relieve cramps and pain. It can be taken externally (as a tincture on wounds) and internally (as tea). Simply mix a handful of the flowers in the feed or half a handful of flowers mixed with a half liter of boiling water.

Valeriana officinalis (valerian)

It is mainly the dried roots of the valerian plant that are used. Valerian has a calming and relaxing effect, without impairing athletic achievement. This is an herb for all kinds of stress-related situations, dental examination being one of them.

A warmblood horse gets a daily dose of 15 grams of ground root. The herb has a most distinctive smell and the dose should be small to start off, in order to accustom the animal to the smell and taste.

Verbena officinalis (European vervain)

All parts of the plant above the ground can be used for a tea that is both calming and boosts the nervous system. It is especially used in general restoration after greater interventions, for it supports the liver function. In Chinese medicine it is also given as "Me Bian Cao" for the harmonizing of the liver. It is an exceptional herb for calming temperamental horses that often "go wild."

Brew a tea of half a liter of boiling water and 20-30 grams of fresh or dried herb and serve over the feed after it has cooled off.

Scutellaria lateriflora (skullcap)

According to traditional Chinese medicine, skullcap relaxes and strengthens the meridians of the heart and the kidneys. The parts of the plant above the ground prepared as a tea will serve well to soothe apprehensive, sensitive and frail animals.

The tea is brewed from a handful of the dried herb and a half a liter of water. Administer three cupfuls per day. Skullcap is also available as a powder that can be sprinkled over the feed (15-20 grams per day).

Bach flower remedies

This method of healing was founded in the 1930s by Dr. Edward Bach. The flower remedies do not act on the body of the patient, but regulate the mental balance of the person or animal that uses them. Horses too have behavior that can be positively influenced by the Bach flower remedies. There are 38 classic Bach flowers that can be effective for different emotional problems. The best approach is to assess the horse according to the characteristics given to the flowers and to administer the flower or flowers that appear to be the most effective. Rockrose, for example, is for shock, fear and panic, while limulus is for animals that are apprehensive in general and are concerned when the blacksmith, veterinarian or any other stranger comes near. Gentian is not one of the classic five fear flowers, but is very effective on horses that are sensitive and insecure and become excited in treatments, while holly is for anger and

jealousy. This last is the flower remedy for aggressive animals whose motto appears to be "the best form of defense is offense" and which are dangerous for everyone involved.

The way a horse is kept and the way it is treated will naturally play a big role in the problems it has. No aggressive horse will become a lamb by just using the Bach flower remedies unless the other problems are ironed out. However, the Bach flower remedies can represent a foundation for change and make change itself possible.

Rescue remedy should in any case always be at hand. This is the only ready-mixed solution of the flower remedies that is available. Rescue remedy contains cherry plum, clematis, impatiens, rockrose and star of Bethlehem. This remedy is to reinstate balance after all kinds of stress, change or fear.

Bach flower remedies are manufactured in their so-called stock bottles. A drop of the remedy from the stock bottle is mixed with ten milliliters of water. A big horse is then given ten drops of this mixture, three to four times daily on a piece of dried bread or in the feed. The rescue remedy is two drops mixed with ten milliliters of water. The more acute the situation, the more often the rescue remedy must be administered. If need be, two to four drops of the pure mix can be administered.

There are many other alternative therapies in holistic veterinary care that should be mentioned here. Reiki, aromatherapy and kinesiology are just a few examples of the many other possibilities. Jen-Hsiao Lin, a fourteenth-century Chinese sage said: "It does not matter if the remedy is old or new, as long as it heals, and it does not matter if the method and its teaching is from the east or west, as long as it is effective."

The welfare of the patient should always be the highest prerogative. As praiseworthy as alternative medicine may be, it cannot replace conventional medicine, especially not when practiced by laypersons.

A great deal can be achieved, however, with the remedies presented in this text.

Book List

Self, Hilary:
A Modern Horse Herbal,
1996, Half Halt Press.

Wilde, Claire:
Hands-on Energy Therapy for Horses and Riders,
1999, Trafalgar Square.

Macleod, George:
The Treatment of Horses by Homeopathy,
1995, CW Daniel Co.

Coates, Margrit:
Healing for Horses,
2002, Sterling.

Grosjean, Nelly:
Veterinary Aromatherapy,
1994, CW Daniel Co.

Ingraham, Caroline:
Aromatherapy for Animals,
2001, Orphans Press.

Brennan, Mary:
Complete Holistic Care and Healing for Horses,
2004, Trafalgar Square.

Scott, Martin J:
Bach Flower Remedies for Horses and Riders,
2000, Kenilworth Press.

Zidonis, Nancy A:
Equine Acupressure, a Working Manual,
1999, Equine Acupressure, Inc..

Instruments for the examination of the mouth

Examination of the horse's mouth is a complicated business. As discussed above, the incisors can be seen and examined with relative ease without the use of any instruments. The examination of the premolars and molars is more difficult. They are far to the back of the mouth and even looking into the depths of the mouth is tricky. Putting a hand into the horse's mouth, to feel the molar teeth without the benefit of some tools would be careless and could lead to the loss of fingers or fingernails.

Some of the instruments that can be used for the examination of the mouth will be discussed in the next pages. These instruments should be used with the greatest care, and preferably by experienced people only.

Safeguarding the horse and the helpers with suitable measures must be a matter of course. In some cases sedation of the horse is necessary, either orally or by injection (see page 101ff). The instruments suggested earlier should be used to thoroughly examine the horse's mouth.

Treatment of diseases in the horse's mouth should be left to professionals. Specialist therapy is not the theme of this book; therefore the specialized therapy and its instruments will not be deliberated upon further.

Headlamp

Successful examination of the horse's mouth is only possible when proper light is available. In order to have both hands free to perform the inspection, it is advised to wear a headlamp. There are various kinds of headlamps with good illumination capacity available commercially.

Thumb wedge

The thumb wedge is available when the mouth needs to be opened slightly and serves as protection for the fingers at the same time. Unfortunately the opening of the mouth that is obtained with the thumb wedge is not enough and fixing the jaw in one place is unreliable. This instrument is suitable for the examination of the premolars.

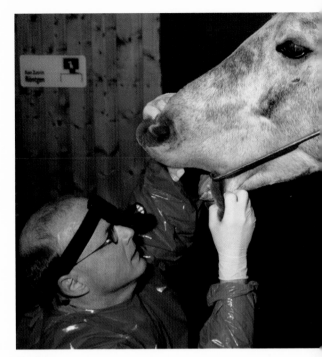

Headlamp

Thumb wedge

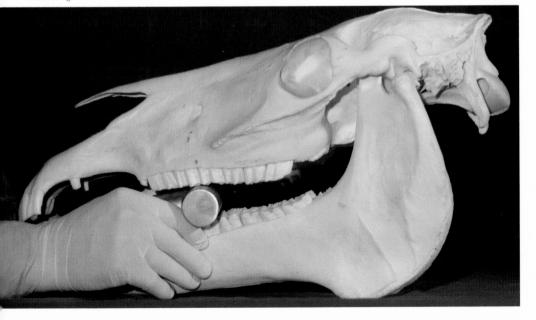

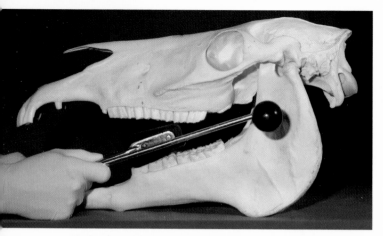

Mouth wedge made from rubber. The danger of injury is reduced with this wedge.

Bayer's mouth wedge (metal wedge)

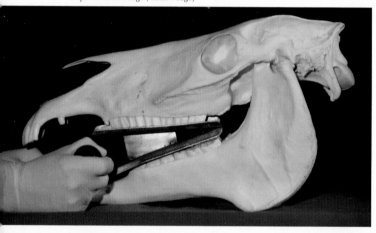

Schoupe's mouth wedge.

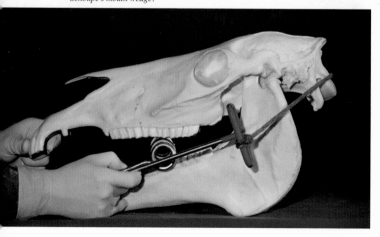

Mouth wedges

The mouth wedge serves the purpose of opening the mouth much better than the thumb wedge. The most important task is stabilizing the wedge between the rows of the molars, without injury to the horse. The best type of mouth wedge has rubber attached to the metal; the rubber can be replaced. Plain metal wedges pose a bigger danger of injury to the mouth of the horse. Sharp edges on the metal can cut the soft tissue and a molar can even be fractured when the horse bites on the metal. The palate can also be damaged, which will lead to profuse bleeding. Opening the mouth is more dependable when these wedges are used, however.

Schoupe's mouth wedge

This wedge looks like an element for boiling water. The biggest danger here is that when a horse bites too hard on it, the pressure on the sides of the teeth might cause fractures. Wedges made from synthetic materials are mostly kinder on the teeth than the metal ones.

Mouth speculum

The mouth speculum, or mouth gag, is perhaps the most recommended alternative for the successful opening of the horse's mouth. It is placed between the incisors, and is a secure way to expose the molars. The danger of the speculum slipping is also minor. The deciding factor is the quality of the speculum. There are speculums made of cast iron that can easily break: too bad when your hand is in the horse's mouth at the time (as experienced by the author!). The forged speculums are much better quality but obviously much more expensive.

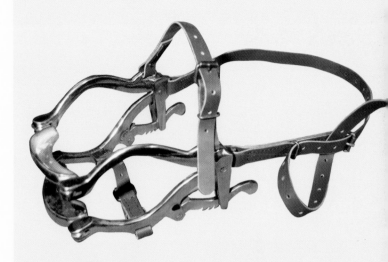

Mouth speculum

Mouth speculum for the examination of the incisors

The above speculum with a different vertical plate can also be used to examine the incisors. The vertical plate is placed behind the canine but in front of the first premolar, in the interdental space.

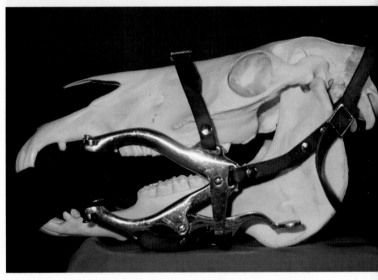

Mouth speculum for inspection of the incisors

Günther's mouth speculum

This mouth speculum is often used when horses are under general anaesthetic, and is not recommended for a general examination. It cannot be tightened properly and can cause serious injury to the assistants and the horse when hurled out of the mouth. Another danger with this speculum is that the spindle provides little feeling for the resistance of the jaw, and the jaw is subsequently opened too wide.

Drenching syringe

The mouth should be rinsed before the dental examination in order to get a good overview of the mouth. There are syringes for this purpose that will not be squashed when the horse accidentally bites on them, and they also contain the appropriate quantity of water. The syringe has a capacity of 300 milliliters. Two or three syringes full of water will rinse most of the food rests out of the mouth to leave it clean for the examination.

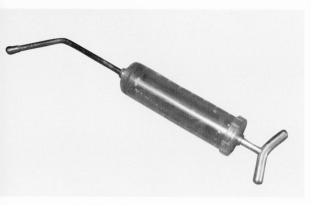

Drenching syringe

Dental picks

Dental pick

Once the mouth is open and rinsed, it is possible to see food rests stuck between the teeth and in the soft tissues. Dental picks can be used to remove these rests.

The dental picks come in different lengths to reach right to the back of the mouth as well.

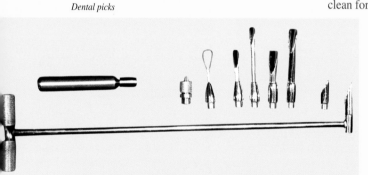

Molar speculum

Molar speculum

This is a simple wickerwork of wire that keeps the cheeks out of the way when the molars are being inspected. With the help of this tool, the chewing surfaces can easily be scrutinized, especially for the assessment of evenness of the chewing surfaces and possible fractures.

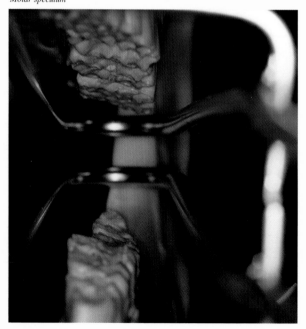

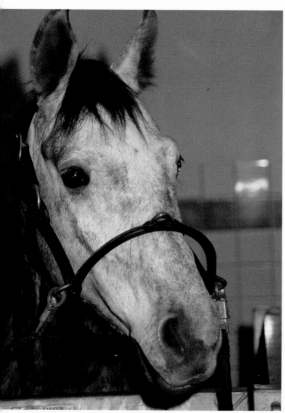

Head collar

Head collar

A big head collar that will not restrict the opening of the mouth will be needed. A professional head collar with an enduring ring around the nose is a very practical benefit. This can be utilized to secure the horse in a position that is comfortable for the examiner.

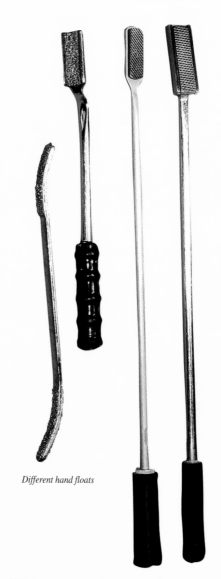

Different hand floats

Hand floats

Different hand floats are shown here for your opinion and appreciation.

The blades for the floats must be particularly hard and sharp because the tooth substance is extremely tough, as already described.

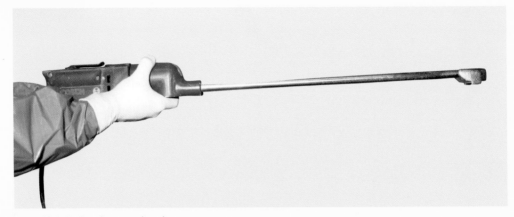

Rotary file for hooks and ramps on the molars

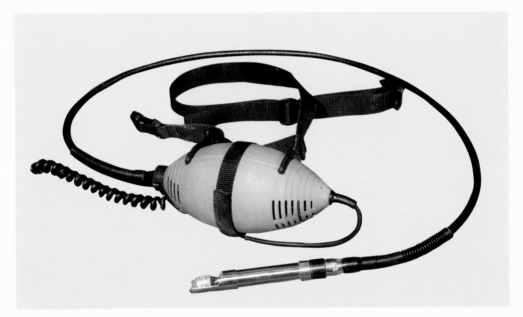

Rotary file for canines and incisors

Wolf tooth elevators

Wolf tooth elevators

These are special tools for the extraction of wolf teeth.

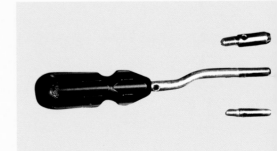

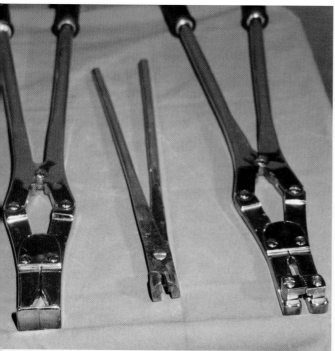

Large extraction forceps

Small extraction forceps

Molar forceps

The removal of molars requires large extraction forceps.

Forceps for the removal of primary tooth caps

Remaining milk teeth and the caps that stay put on the permanent teeth have to be removed manually. These forceps have long or short levers, depending on the position of the teeth. A few examples can be seen below.

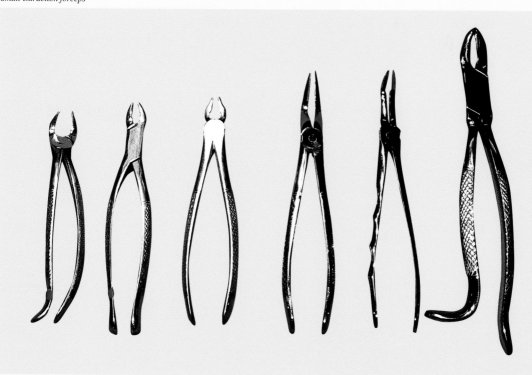

Case Studies

6

The following case studies describe certain symptoms that can suggest disease of the mouth or teeth. Hooks and ramps on the molars and the resulting irritation caused to the tongue or cheeks are always possible reasons for all the described problems. Individual symptoms for other possible causes must be investigated further.

These guidelines are only tips and should not be used as specific strategies to recognize problems in the mouth. Nor should diseases of the teeth be used as an excuse for bad riding! Tooth and mouth ailments must always be ruled out before they become the reason for an argument between horse and rider.

Routine in the practice of the horse dentist

Here are some typical practical examples.

Case study A

"My horse is four years old and was very easy to ride until recently. He now fights against the bit. I have tried various bits and even running reins, but it is only getting worse."

This preliminary report is an everyday occurrence. In most cases a wolf tooth will have erupted, or lies hidden below the level of the gum. Once the reins are taken up, the bit presses against the tooth, and the horse struggles against the pain. Extraction of the wolf tooth is simple and solves the problem easily. Shedding of teeth plays a significant role at this age and can cause noticeable discomfort.

Case study B

"My horse is a jumper in advanced level and is eight years old. On sharp turns he will sometimes come to a standstill and even rear. I have tried reprimanding him but it only gets worse."

This report is not unusual either. Horses' teeth are not always inspected at this age. The first premolar (P2) in the upper jaw and the last molar (M3) in the lower jaw have formed definite hooks. Taking the rein up on one side only will cause tremendous pressure on the tongue, where the hook on the upper premolar presses into it. Floating the hook on the upper

P2 and lower M3 will quickly solve this problem. However, once this problem has resulted in an habitual way of moving, correcting the teeth will not necessarily solve the dilemma. Recognizing it early and correcting the problem will be more effective.

Case study C

"My horse does medium dressage. In collection he fights the bit and shakes his head."

The incisors must be carefully inspected in this case. If the positions of the upper and lower incisors develop differently, this can lead to the incisors being wedged (or locked). When the poll is the highest point in the neck, the lower jaw will be slightly displaced to the front. When this sliding movement is blocked by the wedged incisors, pressure and pain will be the result in the jaw joint. Correction through balancing the chewing surfaces of the incisors can regulate this gliding movement again.

Case study D

"My horse continuously shakes his head. The more demanding I become, the more he shakes his head up and down. Sometimes he puts his nose almost on the ground and does not even move anymore."

This horse is probably a head-shaker. The cause is often difficult to establish and can be diverse.

The maxillary sinuses should be examined. If the

horse reacts when the sinus is tapped, an X-ray will show if an infection of the sinus or the roots of the molars is present. This is very often the problem.

Case study E

"My horse is very restless in her stable. She eats her hay with little enthusiasm and her pellets not at all. I often find balls of hay that have been partially chewed on the floor, and her droppings contain whole grains and other undigested food particles."

Quidding is a classic symptom to watch for. These horses always have distinct ramps on the outside of the upper molars and the inside of the lower molars that can be razor-sharp. These sharp edges can even cut the hand of the examiner. Floating these sharp ramps will usually solve the problem within two to three days. The inflamed mucous membranes of the tongue and the cheeks need this long to heal.

Case study F

"My horse makes a big fuss whenever I want to take the bridle off. He snaps his head up and does not want to release the bit. He is completely normal when ridden."

The incisors and canines do not come into contact with the bit when the horse is ridden. However, when the horse is tacked up, the bit must pass through the incisors. If the area surrounding the inci-

sors is inflamed, it will be uncomfortable for the horse, and he can react in an extreme way. The canines can be an even bigger problem. If there is tartar build-up on the canine, the gum around the tooth can be irritated, and if the bit touches this area, the horse can suffer severe pain. If the canine is sharp, it can also lead to these reactions. To solve the problem, the tartar must be removed, and the tooth be smoothed. Treatment of the inflamed mucous membranes with something like an anti-inflammatory tincture (for example tincture of myrrh) can speed up the healing of the soft tissue.

Case study G

"My horse leans on the rein, is hard in his back and will not let go. He refuses to back, snatches his head up and only steps back reluctantly."

Almost all riders have this problem. It is not always a problem associated with the mouth or teeth. The interdental space must be checked for the existence of a wolf tooth. The first real premolar (P2) must also be checked for a hook on the upper jaw.

The mobility of the lower jaw and the position of the incisors to each other can have a further influence. Horizontal movement of the lower jaw must be possible. The chewing surfaces of the incisors must be balanced to accommodate the movement of the lower jaw against the upper jaw. Pushing on the jaw joint followed by any reaction will indicate the above.

Keywords for the Diagnosis of Mouth and Teeth Problems

Here are some clues to the connection between the symptoms and possible causes in the mouth.

Poor, slow feeding	Ulcers on the palate
	Inflammation of the gingiva
	Inflammation of the tongue
	Tooth fracture
	Inflammation of the socket
Fighting the bit	As above
	Wolf tooth
	Sharp canine
	Inflammation of the bars of the mouth
Struggling to tack up	Inflammation in the incisors
	Sharp canines
	Inflamed tongue
	Injuries to the lips and bars of the mouth

"Back problems" when riding	Uneven wear of the incisors
	Defective position of the jaw
	Lower M3/upper P2 with hooks
	Inflammation of the jaw joint
Head shaking	Inflammation of the maxillary sinus
	Sharp wolf tooth
	Hidden wolf tooth
	Hidden canine
Area around the canines is inflamed	Foreign objects in the tongue
	Injury to the bars of the mouth
Rearing when ridden	Sharp wolf tooth
	Fracture of the lower jaw
	Inflammation in the root of a tooth
	Injury to the bars of the mouth
	Curb chain too tight and too far back
Horse does not back	Foreign objects in the tongue
	Fracture of the lower jaw
	Sharp wolf tooth
	Injury to the bars of the mouth
Horse above the bit	Inflammation of the jaw joint
	Defective position of the jaw
	Inflammation of the upper incisors
Horse behind the bit	Sharp wolf tooth
	Incorrect position of the lower P2
	Inflamed lower interdental space
	Curb chain to tight and too far back

Making faces/swishing the tail	Sharp, hidden wolf tooth
	Hidden canine
	Inflammation of the gingiva
	Defective position of the jaw
	Inflammation of the jaw joint
	Uneven wear of the incisors
Head shy	Tooth fracture
	General inflammation of the mouth
	Inflammation of the sinuses
Big food particles in the droppings	Tooth fracture
	Crooked tooth
	Disease of the chewing muscles
	Inflammation of the jaw joint
Quidding	Tooth fracture
	Foreign body in tongue or gums
	Disease of the chewing muscles
Poor condition	Crooked tooth
	Disease of the chewing muscles
	Tooth fracture
	Inflammation of the jaw joint
Horse eats hay, no pellets	Hooks and ramps
	Inflammation of the mucous membranes
Restlessness in the stable	Different painful situations in the mouth

Foul smell from the mouth	Tooth fracture
	Inflammation of the socket
	Abscess in the mouth
Horse plays with the water	Inflammation in the mouth
	Foreign bodies
	Burned tongue
Bleeding from the mouth	Injury to the tongue or mucous membranes
	Tooth fracture after a kick or blow
	Injury to the socket after a kick or blow
Unilateral runny nose	Sepsis of the maxillary sinus
	Inflammation of the root of an upper molar
Frequent colic or obstruction in the throat	Disturbance of the mechanics of chewing
	Inflammation of the mucous membranes
	Extreme hooks and ramps
	Fractured teeth

Diagnosis of the tooth problem does not solve the predicament. Floating the sharp teeth, removing retained caps and wolf teeth as well as further treatment must be carried out by a veterinarian. There are also dentists for horses that can carry out routine treatment. It is, however, extremely difficult for a horse owner to judge the competence of the examiner. For this reason there are a number of veterinarians who have specialized in this field.

Naturally, your own veterinarian can offer this service or put you in touch with a reliable specialist in this line of work.

Book List

Baker, Gordon J. & Easly, Jack:
Equine Dentistry,
1999, W B Saunders.

Auer, Jorg:
Equine Surgery,
1999, W B Saunders.

Pence, Patricia et al.
Equine Dentistry: A Practical Guide,
2001, Lippincott Williams and Wilkens.

INDEX